The Bud

D0789770
7

Mukunda Rao is the author of works, six books of fiction and two plays. His *Biology of Enlightenment* (HarperCollins, 2001) is a much read and discussed work the world over, and has become a cult book among spiritual aspirants. His play *Baba Saheb Ambedkar*, which had a successful run four years ago, was produced again, this year to critical acclaim. There were altogether ninety-five shows in different parts of Karnataka. After his voluntary retirement from a teaching job in a college in 2000, he now lives with his wife on a farm outside Bengaluru.

Praise for *Between the Serpent and the Rope*

'Your book is a wonder … it reads like a novel; the story-telling is captivating. Yet, it is also part autobiography, part travelogue, part investigative journalism and last but not the least, a deep spiritual exploration churning the teachings of Buddha, Ramana Maharshi and UG.'

– **Narayana Moorty, retired professor of philosophy, USA**

'I found your book, from its first line to the last one, as a testimony to your erudite, incisive, plain, yet magical writing that conveys the intricate yet exquisite agony and ecstasy of a spiritual journey.'

– **Basavaraj Puranik, noted writer in Kannada, Bengaluru**

Praise for *The Other Side of Belief: Interpreting U.G. Krishnamurti*

'This book is intended for all those readers who at some time or the other think of the mystery called life, but it is not for those whose sensibilities get offended easily. Mukunda Rao uses a personal narrative to understand life through that of UG and his unholy utterances. In this strangely shell-shocking yet therapeutic process, the reader is made to question almost all beliefs at the core of one's existence.

For those like me who have been seeking answers, this book comes as a welcome cold shower; a wake-up call to not ignore physical life itself in the quest for the spiritual.'

– Jaydeep Deosthale, *Deccan Herald Sunday*

'In this book Mukunda Rao has been able to capture and report with startling objectivity the essence of an unwilling mystic, U.G. Krishnamurti.

The reader swings between admiration, disbelief, disgust and unwilling faith in what UG arrived at and Rao's style of narration and presentation is as much responsible for this experience as UG's thoughts.'

– E. Jayashree Kurup, *Financial Express Sunday*

'A big WOW, to say the least. A blow to my studies and "intellectual" understanding of the world. But, thank god for it ... it shook me to my core. Interesting, fascinating and true beyond words, which is where I think that it all points – beyond words.'

– Michael McClure, Arizona State University, USA

'My compliments on your courage in writing so well on what must be the most difficult subject of all time!'

– Douglas Rosestone, counselor at Self, California

'Your books are a clear summary of UG's life and they are wonderful to read. I am glad you have so well documented them.'

– Mark Whitwell, teacher and author of
books on Yoga, California

The Buddha

An Alternative Narrative of His Life and Teaching

MUKUNDA RAO

First published in India in 2017 by Harper Element
An imprint of HarperCollins *Publishers*

Copyright © Mukunda Rao 2017

P-ISBN: 978-93-5264-420-9
E-ISBN: 978-93-5264-421-6

2 4 6 8 10 9 7 5 3 1

HarperCollins *Publishers*
A-75, Sector 57, Noida, Uttar Pradesh 201301, India
1 London Bridge Street, London, SE1 9GF, United Kingdom
Hazelton Lanes, 55 Avenue Road, Suite 2900, Toronto, Ontario M5R 3L2
and 1995 Markham Road, Scarborough, Ontario M1B 5M8, Canada
25 Ryde Road, Pymble, Sydney, NSW 2073, Australia
195 Broadway, New York, NY 10007, USA

Typeset in 11/14 Dante MT
by Jojy Philip, New Delhi 110 015

Printed and bound at
Thomson Press (India) Ltd.

Contents

BOOK THREE
Mahasamadhi: The Final Absorption

Preface

In Buddhist scriptures, the body is mostly seen as a source of trouble, an obstacle in the path of spirituality, a burden to be overcome in order to attain enlightenment. Such an attitude towards the body (also to be found in Hindu and other religious texts), compounded by an inadequate knowledge of it in comparison to the mind or soul, probably prevented an understanding of the biological changes involved in altered states of consciousness, especially in the transformation of a human being into an enlightened being.

Unfortunately, the situation has not changed much even today. Spiritual discourses continue to be shrouded in supernaturalism, myth and metaphor, while enlightenment or nirvana is still viewed as separate from the body or unrelated to the body. The body is seen as a sort of 'enemy' that needs to be controlled and disciplined in one's spiritual enterprise.

It is not as if attempts have not been made, either in the past or in the present, to remedy this defective view, but these attempts have been subsumed under discourses that were and are largely framed in psychological terms. Hence, the body continues to be regarded as an obstacle to be overcome in the spiritual quest. This book is an attempt to fill the gap in our understanding of the biological foundation of nirvana.

'Within this fathom-long sentient body itself,' the Buddha maintained, 'are the world, the arising of the world, the cessation of the world and the path leading to the cessation of the world.' In other words, the arising of the world, the self and the cessation of the self and thereby, the cessation of what the Buddha calls 'dukkha', are all within the body.

Extending the metaphor, we may add that within the body is the cosmic dance of life; rather, the cosmos itself is the body. Here, the portrayal of the vishwarupa, the universal form of Lord Krishna as given in the Bhagavadgita, may serve as a brilliant metaphor for the body.

After a rather lengthy discourse on the different forms of yoga and on the nature of Brahman and Atman, Krishna bestows on Arjuna a vision of his *universal form*. Arjuna beholds the whole cosmos reflected in the seamless *body* of Krishna: all the innumerable forms of life exist here, and in the centre is Brahma resting on a lotus, surrounded by sages and heavenly serpents. The sun, the moon and the heavenly planets blaze along; worlds radiate within worlds in a never-ending kaleidoscope; rivers flow relentlessly into thunderous seas. In effect, what the text, rather unwittingly, reveals is that it is not the soul or spirit but the *body* that is immortal; it is boundless, without a beginning, a middle or an end.

The teaching of the Buddha is primarily about the nature and functioning of the mind and about enlightenment, a state of being where all conflicts and fears have ceased, where the divisive mind has gone quiet and the body, now cleansed of destructive passion and re-established in its pristine state, begins to live in a rhythm natural to it and in tune with the cosmos. This is also a state where there is, to use a Biblical phrase, 'peace that passeth understanding'. *This* is the state of being, the answer, the change, the goal that humanity, through its philosophies and religions, has been yearning and struggling for since the beginning of civilization.

It is the spiritual impulse in us that sets up the quest, the search for truth and for enlightenment. During this journey, we pursue knowledge, listen to gurus, do sadhana and meditate. Thus we struggle for years, yet the goal seems to elude us. We realize—if we are ruthlessly honest with ourselves—that after a point, this long, testing journey with all its sadhana and experiences has turned counterproductive. We may sometimes feel we are making progress, getting nearer, almost there ... but it is a delusion: we are only moving in circles. Indeed, it is hard to grasp and difficult to accept that, eventually, it is this spiritual knowledge and sadhana that prevents us from reaching the purported goal of our quest: freedom. To understand and accept this tricky situation, wholly and honestly, would entail *giving up* the spiritual struggle, but we are not prepared for this.

In other words, the state of being where the binary or divisive mind has gone quiet, where dukkha has ended, *is* the freedom we seek. This is the natural state of every human being. But it is a state of being that sadhana cannot take us to, and our mind cannot reach. Knowledge, the product of the mind—which is mind itself—cannot penetrate there, where differentiations don't exist, where there is no duality. It has to give way to something else.

What is that something else? Can the mind ever become quiet? Can anything be understood at all without the mind? What is the nature of the mind and the body? What is suffering?

Can morality change people? What is knowledge? Is there a 'beyond'; is there timelessness?

This narrative examines these timeless existential questions by revisiting and retelling the story of the Buddha. No easy task, given the bewildering number of Buddhist schools and sub-schools, and the extensive literature covering a period of more than sixteen centuries, the sheer complexity and vastness of which can be quite intimidating even to a thoroughgoing scholar. Being neither a scholar nor a philologist, I have approached my task as a seeker.

Drawing from diverse sources such as the Pali canon, Mahayana texts, Zen Buddhism, J. Krishnamurti, Ramana Maharshi, U.G. Krishnamurti, Nietzsche, postmodernist thinkers and the biological sciences, I have tried, using S. Radhakrishnan's expression, 'to wrest from words the thought that underlies them', as I retell the story of the Buddha and discuss his teachings in a language free of metaphysics and mysticism.

In such a work where the subjects discussed intersect continually, repetitions are inevitable. For instance, while talking about the nature and functioning of the mind, body and soul, nirvana or the 'natural state' and so on, certain words and expressions and even quotations from the Pali canon and other texts may turn up again and again, and I hope they will enable one to see things from multiple perspectives and get a sense of the various concepts used. However, we need to bear in mind that all concepts and ideas used in the narrative are not of absolute but of relative and instrumental value; they are only pointers to *that* which cannot be captured in the fishbowl of the mind.

Readers may find some of the quotations, especially from the Pali canon and U.G. Krishnamurti's books, quite lengthy and even distracting, but I believe it's absolutely necessary in such a narrative to give a feel of the original, to let the masters speak directly to us. I have deliberately not used diacritical marks for Sanskrit words, simply because I think it's time we do away with the practice. Most of these words or terms are well known; even otherwise, a serious and discerning reader will surely make efforts to grasp them.

It is quite possible that all my readers may not always agree with my interpretation of the Buddha's teaching, and they may have reservations about my biological interpretation of nirvana in particular. I know this kind of reading of the Buddha's life and teaching is something very different and may even challenge the interpretations put forward over the years by many monks and scholars.

Thirty years of contemplation and sadhana, revisiting the teachings of Ramana Maharshi and other sages and, crucially, my association and conversations with U.G. Krishnamurti, presented me with insights I felt a deep desire to share with others. I sincerely believe it will contribute to our study of the way of the Buddha, and to our understanding of this most enigmatic subject called nirvana.

I will be glad and feel amply recompensed, therefore, if my attempt here is taken forward; I will be doubly glad if it is contested. As T.R.V. Murti, an insightful scholar on Buddhism, says, 'In philosophy, difference of interpretation is legitimate, and should even be welcome.'

Having said that, I rest my case here and record my obligations. It seems I have been contemplating, meditating, wondering and working on the subject of this book for ages. During this journey—at times confounding but eventually illuminating—I benefitted from the suggestions and encouragement of several friends. I owe my grateful thanks to them, especially to Narayana Moorty, my first reader and critic, for his valued criticism and helpful advice. I am greatly indebted to Sundar Sarukkai for his probing questions, which helped me reconsider the text with a fresh, critical eye. I thank James Farley for his careful reading of the text and valuable suggestions as well as Chandrashekar Babu for his generous encouragement.

This is not an easy book to edit, but Rukmini Chawla Kumar has done a remarkable job with her sensitive and balanced editing. I owe many thanks to her. I also thank V.K. Karthika and Ajitha G.S. for their support and for bringing out the book so well.

Mukunda Rao

Bangalore
January 2017

Introduction

The period between 800 and 300 BCE was an era of great transformation in the history of humankind. Recent scholars have termed this period the 'Axial Age' because it proved to be pivotal, especially in the spiritual growth of humanity. It seems that there was an explosion of energy in human consciousness, something analogous to the biological mutation that led to the emergence of Homo sapiens on earth 200,000 years ago.

During this period, in four distinct global regions, the world witnessed the presence of powerful masters: in Iran, the rise of Zoroaster; in India, the sages of the Upanishads (500–400 BCE), Mahavira (468 BCE) and the Buddha (563–483 BCE); in Israel and Palestine, the Hebrew prophets; in China, Confucius (551–479 BCE) and Lao-tzu (sixth century BCE); and, in Greece, Pythagoras (582–500 BCE), Heraclitus (500 BCE), Socrates (469–399 BCE) and Plato (427–347 BCE).[1] Their penetrating insights into the human condition and the nature of reality triggered a shift in human consciousness. The result was the development of new religions and philosophical systems that continue to challenge and inspire humanity to this day. This narrative, however, focuses on the Buddha, for in his life and teaching, in the full awakening of the human being, we witness the culmination of centuries of spiritual development.

As you will probably know, 'Buddha' was not a name as such, but became the term for the person who was once called Siddhartha Gautama. 'Buddha' means the one who has awakened from ignorance and is free from fear and desire, from gods and goals, from a dualistic mode of living in the world. The Buddha is he who functions in the state of nirvana or what U.G. Krishnamurti calls the 'natural state'.

But what was this Buddha like? How was he different from Siddhartha Gautama, the son of King Suddhodana? Was he a superman? Was he a 'mutant', an avatar or a sage like Ramana Maharshi and U.G. Krishnamurti? Was he the dry, humourless person he is often portrayed to be in traditional texts? Did he believe in reincarnation? Did he really start the sangha of bhikkhus and encourage conversions?

It may be difficult to imagine what the Buddha was actually like as a person but it is not impossible. The sources we have for our study are the numerous discourses and legends of the Buddha as found in the Pali canon, *Lalitavistara* (third century CE), *Nidanakatha* (fifth century CE) and Ashvaghosha's *Buddhacharita* (second century CE). These works are embellished with supernatural events and mythical and metaphysical narratives, but they are thankfully also interspersed with the more mundane and historically probable events of the Buddha's life. It is indeed tricky to pinpoint and assert that this is exactly how the Buddha lived, moved and taught. Yet, reading between the lines, and in the light of the teachings and lives of sages, it is possible to ascertain and discard elements that could not have been a part of the Buddha's life and teaching. Then, one can arrive at a fairly balanced and credible view of this great, awe-inspiring being who walked more than 2,600 years ago.

Buddhavachana

Three months after the passing away of the Buddha, under the patronage of King Ajatashatru, about 500 monks are believed to have held a council at Rajagriha in order to recall and collate the Buddhavachana, the Buddha's words. The council was convened by Mahakasyapa, one of the chief disciples of the Buddha who became the leader of the community of monks after the Buddha's death.

In this extraordinary gathering of Buddhist monks, legend holds that a monk called Upali, who had complete knowledge of the Buddha's rules of monastic conduct, presented these rules to the assembly. Ananda, cousin and constant companion of the Buddha for more than thirty years and known for his prodigious memory, recited all of the Buddha's sermons. The council devised a system of communal recitation, what is generally called an oral tradition, to retain and pass on the teaching.

Then it was only in the first century BCE in Sri Lanka that the discourses were written down in Pali in the form of anthologies. These anthologies were referred to as Tripitaka, the three 'baskets' or collections of the Buddha's words: Sutta Pitaka, the basket of Discourses; Vinaya Pitaka, the basket of Disciplines; and Abhidamma Pitaka, the basket of Higher Knowledge, containing philosophical and doctrinal analyses of the teaching.

About a hundred years later, the second council was held at Vesali. This was mainly to discuss certain serious differences that arose within the Buddhist order over the practices and interpretations of the Buddha's teachings. The orthodox followers of the Buddha believed that the monks of Vaisali were taking liberties with the rules prescribed in the Vinaya Pitaka. The council discussed the matter at length but could not reach an agreement. This resulted in a great schism within the order and led to the formation of two divergent schools: the Sthaviravadins, who advocated a strict adherence to the early tradition of Buddhism and compliance with the 'original' teachings of the Buddha; and the Mahasamghikas, who did not find any problem in having a liberal attitude towards the rules prescribed in the Pitakas.

The third Buddhist council (250 BCE) was held under the Mauryan King Ashoka at Pataliputra. The fourth one (first to second centuries CE) took place in Kanishka, the fifth (1871) and the sixth (1954) in Burma (Myanmar). With the exception of the first council, the later councils were ridden with controversies, a conflict of interests, allegations of corruption and deviations from the original path laid down by the Buddha; in short, a betrayal of the Buddhavachana. Given the history of religions and the creation of different sects in every religion over time, it is unsurprising that so many Buddhist councils had to be held over the centuries, where *the way* was doctrinally split into innumerable sects, each one claiming to be true to the Buddhavachana.

Each Buddhist sect or school used—and continues to use— the canonical texts to suit its teaching. In the fifth and sixth centuries, some of these texts were translated into Sanskrit, Chinese and Tibetan. Even though it is claimed that these texts are records of the Buddha's words, interpolations were inevitable. An interpolation, in relation to ancient manuscripts, is an entry or passage in a text that was not written or said by the original author. There is a natural tendency for extraneous material to be inserted into such texts over long periods of time, and this is how all scriptures have been handed down from generation to generation, with the psychological and cultural needs and aspirations of people of different periods worked into them. But then, as it happens, any scripture or teaching is already an 'interpolation', rather, already an interpretation; there is no escaping that fact.

BUDDHIST SCHOOLS

It is important to note here that Buddhists of different sects or schools who claimed to represent and follow the way of the Buddha in different countries, for instance, in Sri Lanka or China, did not think they shared a single faith or religion until Western scholars coined the term 'Buddhism' in the 1830s to refer to the teachings of the Buddha. The label stuck and became an umbrella term under which we recognize today numerous Buddhist sects/schools of thought, each with its own doctrine and method, each claiming to be the correct interpretation of the teachings of the Buddha and, therefore, the correct path to nirvana and the emancipation of humankind at large. However, among these different schools, while some laid emphasis on faith and devotion to the Buddha and looked upon the Buddha as a personal god, others advocated meditation and wisdom as the means to nirvana. Over time, these different schools were brought under the three 'yanas': Hinayana, Mahayana and Vajrayana, supposedly representing three vital stages in the teachings of the Buddha.

Hinayana, the 'small way' or 'inferior vehicle' is also called the Theravada school or School of Elders. Its doctrines and methods are supposed to be based on the Pali canon (the canon being already heavily influenced by the Theravada school) and is widely practised in Sri Lanka, Myanmar, Thailand, Cambodia and Laos. Mahayana, the 'great way' or 'superior vehicle', its literary basis being the texts of the Chinese and Tibetan sacred canon (the majority of which are believed to be translations from the Sanskrit originals, but now lost) prevails in Nepal, China, Japan, Mongolia, Korea and parts of Central Asia. Mahayana developed as a reaction to Hinayana's conservative, scholastic and 'negative' approach to nirvana and its overemphasis on celibacy and monasticism. Discarding what were seen as the extreme positions of Hinayana, Mahayana grew to be a progressive and liberal branch of Buddhism. Its particular appeal lay in its ideal of the Bodhisattva, which is considered by many to be the heart of Buddhism. It is probably the most popular form of Buddhism today, especially in the West, given its accent on wisdom and compassion.[2]

Vajrayana or the 'diamond vehicle', otherwise called the 'adamantine way', belongs to the Tantra School of Buddhism. It is predominantly what is called 'yogic-magical' in character and lays great emphasis on sadhana with vigour and determination. Philosophically, Vajrayana is closer to Mahayana, yet it differs from it and from the other schools in its emphasis on sunyata or the 'Buddha nature' not just as a psychological phenomenon but, more importantly, as a physical and physiological phenomenon. In short, in Vajrayana, the attainment of nirvana means the transmutation of the body. Hence, the Buddha or Buddha nature is described in terms of Trikayas or the three bodies: Nirmanakaya, the body that manifests in time and space; Sambhogakaya, the body of mutual enjoyment; and Dharmakaya, the body of the Tathagata or the reality body, which embodies the very principle of enlightenment and knows no limits or boundaries. Sometimes, the Buddha is also described as Svabhavikakaya, which means the unity of the three kayas.[3]

Despite these differences and a divergence of doctrines and methods, the unity of these three very different schools of Buddhism consists in the fact that they all aim at enlightenment, at rediscovering, reproducing or recreating the Buddha nature.

PURANA'S DOUBT

A story goes that after the death of the Buddha in Kusinara (modern Kushinagar, Uttar Pradesh), a group of disciples met at Rajagriha. After deliberations that lasted several months, Purana, one of the Buddha's oldest disciples, was invited to this group and asked to approve and accept the canon. Purana declined, saying, 'The Canon of the Doctrine and the Law, my friends, has been admirably fixed by the elders, but I will adhere to that which I have myself heard and received from the Exalted One.' The elders made no reply.[4]

We are not in Purana's position, distanced as we are from the Buddha by more than 2,600 years. And we are not even sure if the Pali canon is authentic. But we know these texts largely reflect the viewpoint of the Theravada school, which is not necessarily an objective view of the Buddha and his teachings. We also know that there are 'elements in it which are certainly the result of later thought and possibly also elements older than the Buddha, which though not included by him in the teaching, were afterwards incorporated in it by his followers responsible for the canon'.[5]

So, one may then ask: Is it possible to come face-to-face with the Buddha outside these traditions?

It is not possible if we view the Buddha as a mere historical figure who said what he said, and is now dead and gone. But if he is a living phenomenon, 'immortal' in the sense that what he said, what he discovered and the state of being he came into are something that can be rediscovered here and now—indeed, have been rediscovered and realized by sages over the centuries (though their expressions of that state of being may differ)—it is not impossible.

Religious traditions can both be productive and counterproductive depending upon our reading. All traditions carry within them elements that can break through the existing framework and open up new ways of seeing and perceiving what is there, without getting caught in the web of concepts and symbols—provided, of course, we approach them with an open, unbiased mind.

A CAVEAT

Once, emphasizing the purely instrumental and relative nature of the Dharma, which was actually the nature of all concepts used by him, the Buddha said:

'Monks, using the figure of a raft, I will teach you the Dhamma [in Pali] as something to leave behind, not to take with you. Listen and pay close attention.'

'As you say, Lord,' the monks responded to the Blessed One.

The Blessed One said, 'Suppose a traveller, after covering a long distance, reaches a river and wishes to cross over to the other shore. But, with neither a ferryboat nor a bridge going from this shore to the other, a thought occurs to him that he could himself build a raft to cross the river. Gathering grass, twigs, branches and leaves he builds a raft with the help of which he crosses the river. Now, having reached the other shore, suppose the traveller were to think, "How useful this raft has been to me! For it was in dependence on this raft that I have crossed over to safety on the further shore. Why don't I hoist it on my head or carry it on my back wherever I go?"

'What do you think, monks? Would the man, in doing that, be doing what should be done with the raft?'

'Surely not, Lord.'

'And what should the man do in order to be doing what should be done with the raft? He would think, "All right, this raft has been helpful to me to cross the river, now let me drag it on dry land or sink it in the water and leave it there and go my way."

'In the same way, monks, I have taught the Dhamma for the purpose of crossing over, not for the purpose of holding onto. Understanding the Dhamma as taught compared to a raft, you should let go even of Dhammas, to say nothing of non-Dhammas.'[6]

Accordingly, all concepts and ideas in this narrative possess not an absolute but only a relative value. What we are going to say about the Buddha and other sages and their teachings should be, therefore, understood in the spirit of the parable of the raft: they are only pointers or signposts, not a road map.

BOOK ONE

Tathagata

One Who Has Thus Gone

Going Forth

By the time Siddhartha Gautama (or Siddhatta Gotama as he is called in Pali) came of age, power from the tribal republics of north India had begun to shift to centralized monarchies. The essentially rural society was giving way to Iron Age technology. A market economy had begun to develop and spread, where merchants, businessmen and bankers emerged as the new power brokers. In the east of the Gangetic plain, cities like Varanasi, Rajagriha and Champa were burgeoning trade centres, and in these cities, the Buddha would teach his revolutionary way to enlightenment. In the western part of the Gangetic plain, the great insights of the Upanishadic seers were still underground, shared and debated only amongst initiates. However, the concepts of samsara, avidya, karma, atman and moksha had spread by this time and were widely discussed. The Buddha was to incorporate some of these ideas into his teaching but contest the key concept of atman, which challenged many a spiritual tradition that existed at the time.

Wandering sanyasis in ochre robes, yogis sitting in padmasana, rapt in meditation or tapas, offering their teachings as a way out of sorrow, were a familiar sight. Renunciation or pabbajja, a Pali term that means 'going forth in search of truth', was seen as the highest ideal one could aspire to, long before young Gautama left home to work his own way to nirvana.[1]

Gautama's father, Suddhodana, who is traditionally referred to as a king of the Sakyas, a scion of the solar race, was probably a minor king or the head of a small republic. His wife was called Maya, it is said, because of her resemblance to Maya the Goddess; her name had nothing to do with the concept of maya.

Queen Maya had set her heart on going to Lumbini when the time of her delivery approached. There, in a glorious grove that resembled the garden of Chitraratha in Indra's paradise, she gave birth to Gautama. The legend recounts that befitting a Buddha, the child emerged from his mother's right side without causing her pain or injury. He was so lustrous and steadfast that it appeared as if the sun itself had come down to earth. Right after his birth, he walked seven steps—long, firm strides—like the seven seers. On the seventh day, Queen Maya, unable to bear the joy she felt at the sight of her son's majesty, died and went to dwell in heaven. The prince grew up under the care of Maya's sister, Mahaprajapati.

We are told that the Brahmins, summoned by King Suddhodana, examined the child's body for marks of distinction and predicted that the child would become either a Buddha or a chakravarti, a universal king. The seer, Asita, apparently broke down in tears on seeing the child. When the king asked why he was crying and if something was wrong with the child, Asita said, 'I have absolutely no doubt that this child will become an enlightened being and reveal to the world the way out of sorrow. I'm crying because I will not be there to see it.'

King Suddhodana naturally preferred his son being a chakravarti rather than a spiritual master. Thus, he made arrangements to ensure that Gautama lived a completely sheltered life and was never exposed to anything that could affect his mind and lead him to the path of sanyasa. When he grew up, Gautama was married to the chaste and beautiful Yashodhara, who bore him a son named Rahula.

DISILLUSIONMENT WITH SAMSARA

Gautama's early life was spent in an atmosphere of sensuality and lavish luxury, hardly suited to his contemplative temperament. The one destined to become the Buddha had to first taste a life of pleasure and experience samsara before he embarked upon his spiritual journey.

He had no idea what lay on the other side: dukkha, pain and dissatisfaction, an inescapable part of human condition. King Suddhodana had done his best to shield his son from this reality but the gods had other plans. All creation yearned for the coming of the one who would bring life to its fruition. Gautama just needed a little nudge to begin to question the false securities of pleasure and power, to experience the disgust with life that was necessary to initiate his release from the shackles of samsara so that he could transcend the human condition.

One day, feeling like an elephant locked up inside a barn, the young prince suddenly longed to see the world beyond his gates. He asked Chandaka, his charioteer, to prepare his chariot, and the two of them rode out of the palace. Following King Suddhodana's orders, the main avenue remained clear of all disturbing sights: cripples, beggars, and the old and infirm had been driven away so that their presence would not agitate the prince's untainted mind.

Thus the sight that met Gautama's eyes was one of pure happiness and innocence. The street was lined with healthy and handsome young men and women in colourful clothes and shining jewels. Children ran about laughing. It was a scene of such pleasure that Gautama's heart swelled with pride and joy. 'Jai! Jai! Here comes our great prince!' cried the crowd, and young women tore fresh flowers from their hair and tossed them at Gautama. A plump, middle-aged woman, bejewelled and draped in shining silks, shouted, 'O, the Prince looks like the Sun God come down on earth! Happy, indeed, his wife!'[2]

But who can thwart the will of the gods? Over the next three days, they sent Gautama's way sights that would easily shatter his illusions. On the first day, as the prince enjoyed the company of his happy subjects, an old man appeared nearby, his skin dark and shrivelled, his back bent with the load of many years. He cried, 'Good citizens of Kapilavastu, take pity and give way to an old man. I don't have many days to live.' He clutched at a worn staff to prop up his quavering limbs. A retching cough broke from his wasted body and he trembled like an old shack caught in a storm.

Gautama could not take his eyes off the old man and asked Chandaka to stop the chariot. Then he asked, 'Who is that man there? Is something wrong with him?'

Chandaka said, 'Prince, that is old age, the destroyer of youth and vigour. Once he was like us, erect and healthy, with strength in his limbs. Now all that is gone, devastated by old age, reduced to mere skin and bone; he is a shrivelled image of what he was in his youth.'

'Does it happen to all?' asked Gautama. 'Will this happen to me, to my son, my wife, and to all those near and dear to me?'

'Without doubt,' replied Chandaka, feeling sad for the

prince. 'Neither king nor beggar can escape old age, if one were to live long enough.'

Chandaka's reply was like a thunderbolt. Gautama said, 'How could I have been so ignorant all these years? Turn back, Chandaka, I have seen enough. Let's go home.'

On the second day, unable to contain his curiosity to know more of the outside world, Gautama went out again with Chandaka. This time he beheld a man afflicted by disease. And on the third day, as fate would have it, he came across a corpse being borne along to the burial ground, his family and friends wailing as they accompanied him. Chandaka's answer, 'This, My Lord, is the final end of all beings,' struck Gautama like lightning, tearing his heart asunder.

After being exposed to facets of life he did not know existed, after letting sorrow penetrate his being, Gautama withdraws into himself. Suddenly, there is no joy in living and the life he has lived so far seems a sham, an escape from the realities of life. He tells himself, 'It is not that I despise the objects of senses, for I know full well that they make up what we call samsara. And I know now that nothing is permanent in this world: pain must follow pleasure and it is an inescapable part of the human condition. But I do not know if there is a life beyond this triad of old age, illness and death. If it is not there, clearly this life is one long, extended misery, but if there is something beyond, I must find out what it is.'

Of this stage of Gautama's life, almost every writer paints a grim picture of the young prince's state—how profoundly depressed he was when he began to confront the realities of illness, old age and death. It is hard to believe that King Suddhodana could have succeeded in shutting his son off completely from the outside world. It is also difficult to believe that Gautama would have naively accepted the belief that life was one extended, uninterrupted haven of peace and tranquillity. Hence, he must have known pleasure and pain, anxiety and disappointments, and may have even heard of sramanas renouncing the worldly life and going in search of truth.

But, clearly, the turning point in his life was the sudden recognition of the harsh realities of life. The scenes he witnessed dramatized and marked his conversion, eventually opening him up to the 'near-death experience' that changed the course of his life.³ A close reading of the text suggests to me that it was this life-altering, near-death experience that finally set him up in pursuit of nirvana.

NEAR-DEATH EXPERIENCE

One day, hoping a visit to the countryside might bring him some peace, Gautama rode out on his splendid horse, Kanthaka. He went deep into the countryside and there saw a ploughed field, the soil broken by furrows that looked like rippling water. Tufts of young grass lay scattered here and there and the field was littered with tiny creatures, some wounded, others dead. Gautama alighted from his horse and walked slowly over the ploughed field, overcome with grief at the sight of death.

Then he went and sat under a roseapple tree. There was a quiet breeze, and the leaves of the tree shook gently, as if in agreement with what he was feeling. Gautama began to see in his mind the origination and passing away of all that lives, the impermanence of things. It was not a vision or a product of discursive thinking but a tremendous insight. Somehow, without any effort, he had penetrated into the nature of things.

Gautama then entered a state of consciousness hitherto unknown to him. He was now neither glad nor grieving, and all anxiety and doubt disappeared. Something had changed and things would never be the same again. He rose from the spot, his body-mind charged with a vigour he had not thought possible.

Today, the term 'near-death experience' (NDE) refers to a broad range of personal experiences associated with impending death: a sense of detachment from the body; an experience of absolute dissolution; a powerful sense of serenity, security or warmth; the presence of a light, and so on. These near-death experiences may take place either spontaneously or be induced by certain circumstances or drugs. However, what is of interest to note here is that during such an experience, it seems that there is an opening into a different level of consciousness where a larger reality, transcending time, space and matter, encompasses ordinary reality. This 'opening' may later lead one to deeper mystical experiences; on the other hand, the effect of the experience may disappear completely in due course. In many cases, a near-death experience may just be a traumatic, mind-boggling experience and remain just that, without causing any fundamental or significant change in a person's life.

In the case of the Buddha as well as with other sages like Ramana Maharshi and U.G. Krishnamurti, the near-death experience is of a totally different order. It is a prelude to the real 'death experience', that is, the death of the *self* or the experiencing structure, which catapults a person into the state of enlightenment.

We cannot, of course, assert with any certainty that this is how things happen in the lives of the sages. But we do see a certain pattern in their lives, which gives credence to the idea that the near-death experience is what sets up a potential sage on the path to enlightenment. It is not necessary that whoever undergoes such an experience is bound to attain nirvana. Nevertheless, it is a tremendous experience that can change a person's very perception of life. In more specific terms, it can break the grip of the self, giving one a glimpse of the unitary movement of life.

It is in this sense that the occurrence under the roseapple tree may be characterized as a near-death experience; this experience, unsurprisingly, is analogous to Ramana Maharshi's near-death experience at the age of sixteen.[4] After this, Ramana Maharshi was no more the person he had been. As though under the guidance of some divine power, he proceeded to the foothills of Arunachalam where he attained mukti. I am also reminded of U.G. Krishnamurti's near-death experience in 1953, which set him up on his inner journey and eventually led him into the 'natural state'.

Buddhist texts do not call what happened to the Buddha a 'near-death experience', though they all concur that it was a life-altering experience that gave the young Gautama a glimpse of the transcendental state of being. It was such a powerful experience that, years later, after having gone through several kinds of sadhanas and still unable to come upon nirvana, Gautama noted that this experience held the clue to the state of enlightenment. Some days after this recollection, Gautama did achieve enlightenment.

While some texts place Gautama's near-death experience much before his marriage to Yashodhara, when he was a mere boy, others place it later in his life but before his exposure to the realities of illness, old age and death. Only a few texts declare that the episode occurred *after* the exposure. However, it is quite likely that this came upon him after his encounter with the corpse or some such traumatic experience. Still, what is of critical importance here is that the near-death experience was the turning point in Gautama's life.

RENUNCIATION

Unlike Mahavira who renounced his family life with the consent of his father, Gautama had to creep away in secret because he knew his father would never have consented, let alone Yashodhara. But, before taking the extreme step, legend says that Gautama did make an attempt to get his father's permission to leave. One day he said, 'Father, Your Majesty, this life is not for me. I must leave. This is something I have to do.'

The king couldn't believe his ears and trembled like a tree struck by an elephant. He took his son's hands in his and said, 'You are still young and your son is only a child. This is not the time for you to be turning to religion. You shall not go.'

The king believed Gautama would never disobey him. But Gautama had made up his mind and he could not help going against his father's authority; he would, of course, go on to break all forms of authority, especially that of religion, to free himself from all imposition and conditioning.

And so, in the early hours when all were in deep sleep, his mind straight as an arrow, Gautama went and roused Chandaka. 'Quick, Chandaka, get Kanthaka out. I'm leaving.' And on the beautiful white steed they rode out of town swiftly. Twilight lay on the landscape like a melancholic song when they stopped outside the town in a grove.

Gautama alighted from his steed. And then the enormity of the situation seemed to dawn upon Chandaka, who asked Gautama, 'Why, My Lord, why are you doing this? Your father was right. You are too young to tread this path that is hard to cross, difficult to tread.'

'Indeed this path is hard to cross, difficult to tread,' Gautama agreed. 'But, Chandaka, there is no such thing as a wrong time to take to this path. There is, in fact, no wrong time for truth.'

'What will I tell your father? And what is to become of me?'
Chandaka burst into tears.

The Buddha-to-be said, 'Chandaka, haven't you seen birds
settle on a tree for a while and then go their separate ways again?
Likewise, the meeting of all living beings must inevitably end
in going their separate ways. Now stop this crying and return
to Kapilavastu.'

'But, My Lord,' Chandaka continued tearfully, 'what will I
tell all those who hold you dear to their hearts, what will I tell
your wife and son?'

'Tell them and my father that there is no reason to grieve for
one who has left for the homeless life so as to bring all sorrow
to an end. And tell them that one day I shall return and return
a Buddha.'

Kanthaka shed hot tears too, for he knew the master was
leaving them. Gautama stroked him and said with smile, 'My
dear Kanthaka, weep not. You are not a human to grieve this
way. You should know better.'

Gautama drew his bejewelled sword from its sheath and,
with a single stroke, severed his topknot. He took off his princely
jewels and tossed them aside. Chandaka quickly picked up and
held them close to his chest, his eyes brimming with tears. He
gazed at Gautama, now divested of his princely attire, with a
reverence he had never felt before even for his king.

The End of the Search

Gautama was twenty-nine years old when he renounced the world. He became a sramana, tonsured and clad in the yellow robes that signified his separation from worldly life. Being a sramana meant renouncing his affiliation to caste, family and native land, and enduring all the hardships that came his way. But he could not have started out on his own sadhana straightaway; he had to first learn about the different spiritual paths to freedom and receive spiritual guidance and training before striking out on his own. Thus he went in search of a guru.

Like the Upanishadic tradition of the western Gangetic plain, the sramana tradition on the eastern side of the Ganges did not rely on divine aid or an external agency in its search for truth and freedom. In the Upanishadic search, Vedic mantras, rituals and gods were left behind with the awareness that 'liberation', if there is such a thing, could not possibly be attained through mantras and rituals.

The Upanishadic tradition had reset the spiritual clock. What is closest or always available at hand is one's own self, one's own mind. One has to begin with the self, going within to search for that by which and in which the world exists and moves. Here, it needs to be pointed out that the world of the Upanishads does not portray Brahmins as seekers—they were more involved in chanting Vedic mantras and performing sacrifices—but largely non-Brahmin and 'rebel-Brahmin' sanyasis. These people dared to leave the security of their hearth, turning away not only from samsara but also its gods so that they could turn to themselves and turn *into* themselves. It is in this sense that the Upanishads marked not the last part but the *end* of the Vedas: vedasya antah, Vedanta.

There were certain trends or thought processes in the Vedas that were carried over in the Upanishadic search for truth, but such continuities are true in all forms of cultural and philosophical development, for there can never be a complete disjunction between the past and the present. Every significant cultural and philosophical movement is at once a creative continuity and a radical departure from the past. Therefore, there is nothing in the area of culture, religion or philosophy that can be said to be exclusively Brahminical, Vedic, non-Vedic or Buddhist, or ancient or medieval. Thoughts take on different forms and colours, different avatars as it were, from the beginning of time.

Therefore, the power to deliver oneself from sorrow and come upon freedom lies within one's own being. Consciousness holds the key to unlock the doors to truth. Gautama took to this path like a foregone conclusion. No prayers, pointless rituals and sacrifices; no fear or sin or love. Beyond good and evil, the gaze is turned upon oneself and into the depths of one's own being.[1]

In such an approach, you do not ask the whys and wherefores of evil and suffering, for you know they have no independent and permanent existence; hence you know they can be brought to an end. If evil and suffering have an independent and permanent existence, life will be a never-ending battle between good and evil. And happiness and goodness will involve a perpetual struggle to subdue or repress evil. Another way out of suffering is to try and surrender to an external agency or God, in the hope that that will end your misery.

The Upanishads and the sramana tradition do not make such assumptions: there is no belief in the independent existence of evil or in an external agency. Instead, they consider such a view of life to be conditioned by avidya, ignorance, and the dual nature of the mind; it is all manomaya, made by the mind. The mind perceives reality in terms of duality: joy and sorrow, good and evil, life and death, and this is an error. It is this defect in perception that needs to be corrected in order to neutralize conflict and suffering. Reflecting upon this sramana tradition, Nietzsche wrote:

> It is a hundred times more realistic than Christianity—it has the heritage of a cool and objective posing of problems of its composition; it arrives after a philosophical movement lasting hundreds of years; the concept of 'God' is already abolished by the time it arrives ... it no longer speaks of the struggle against sin but, quite in accordance with actuality, the struggle against suffering. It already has—and this distinguishes it profoundly from Christianity—the self-deception of moral concepts behind it and it stands, in my view, beyond good and evil.[2]

What Nietzsche said is true and yet not entirely true. Across the centuries, there have been examples of mystics and sages in both Christian and Islamic traditions who have spoken not of the struggle against sin but of the struggle against suffering, and spoken in a language beyond good and evil. These radical voices were marginalized by orthodoxies over the centuries, but they are still very much there, waiting to be heard.

The situation in India has been different because of the religious and philosophical development and training over hundreds of years, especially in the Gangetic plains. This exposure prepared the Indian mind to undergo the psychological mutation necessary to move beyond binaries. More importantly, it was the freedom of thought, a free market of ideas nurtured over centuries in India but lacking in other great civilizations at the time, that enabled the Indian enlightenment traditions to break through their own traditional shackles and move beyond good and evil, and even beyond the need for God.

However, later, like the post-Upanishadic traditions, Buddhist traditions that developed centuries after the Buddha's passing away also borrowed the ideas of God/gods, heaven and hell and such metaphysical concepts from popular, God-centred traditions. All the same, the Hindu enlightenment traditions accorded such metaphysical concepts a position below jnana and Brahman, while Buddhists accorded them a position below Buddhadhatu or 'Buddha nature'.[3]

It was a hard life for a sramana, filled with fear, doubt and danger as he walked through inhospitable and dangerous wilderness, sleeping in mountain caves and under trees, surviving by begging for food from kind householders when he reached a town. Yet Gautama took to this path. Sramanas preferred to live in the outskirts of cities, and so Gautama travelled along the outskirts of Magadha and Kosala to meet with them. He queried seekers about their gurus and their approaches to spiritual realization.

There were various spiritual paths and gurus for Gautama to pick from. It is said that at the time, there were about sixty-two different theories of existence and ways to attain enlightenment. The Ajivakas were followers of Makkali Gosala and Purana Kasyapa, who challenged the current theory of karma but still believed in a kind of determinism. The Charvakas were materialists and denied the theory of karma and rebirth as well. The idea of transmigrating souls, they argued, was an invention of a feverish mind. There were no souls; human beings were wholly physical creatures and they would simply return to the elements after death. So the Charvakas maintained that instead of seeking something that did not exist, people would be better off seeking whatever gave them pleasure and peace of mind.

Then there were the sceptics, led by Sanjaya, who were agnostics of sorts, and believed that the very notion of truth was problematic; rather, they maintained that all notions of truth were relative and therefore the search for absolute truth was futile. The best thing, therefore, for one to do was to cultivate such karmas that would foster goodwill and happiness.[4]

Two thousand six hundred years ago, the Indian mind was already engaged in tackling what even today are considered hard questions in philosophy and psychology. Discussions were taking place on topics like the nature of the world and the self, the distinction of the soul, mind and body, and the possibility of an afterlife. Further, if some were busy building elaborate metaphysical theories, others were equally busy demolishing them. Amidst all this serious and incisive probing, there were 'stupid men' who sought to 'purify their persons by diverse modes of austerity and penance', who performed tapas standing on one leg or inhaling smoke or gazing at the sun to overcome the mind, and those who adored and worshipped animals like cows, deer, horses, hogs, monkeys and elephants.[5]

Thus, there was a tremendous explosion and clash of ideas: dialecticians, controversialists, materialists, sceptics, transcendentalists, advocates of immanence and advaita, complementing, contradicting and cancelling yet deepening each other's inquiries. It was a veritable bazaar of beliefs and ideas, which, in varied ways, exists in India to this day. It was an accepted norm at that time, as it is even today in India, for a seeker to find a guru or an alternative path if he found himself dissatisfied with an existing guru and his teaching.

By then, Jainism was already an established religion. Vardhaman, supposedly the last of the Jinas and codifier of the faith, formally known as Mahavira, the great hero or conqueror, was about sixty-one years old when Gautama, at twenty-nine, started his career as a sramana. It is believed that both Mahavira and the Buddha preached on a hill in Rajagriha. So it is quite likely that moving around in Saranath, the Buddha and Mahavira would have heard of each other and might even have crossed each other's paths, like the two modern sages of our time, J. Krishnamurti, and U.G. Krishnamurti would on a street in Gstaad, Switzerland in 1968: two large ships crossing each other in the silence of the dark waters. J. Krishnamurti was seventy-three years old at the time and U.G. Krishnamurti twenty-three years younger.[6]

It is strange and intriguing, therefore, that there should hardly be any reference to Mahavira and Jainism in the Pali canon.[7] Far from entering into unnecessary and fruitless polemics with them, it seems that the Buddha and the Buddhist traditions consciously and deliberately avoided any engagement with other enlightenment traditions. Also, it seems they took care not to couch the Buddhavachana in the language of these traditions, especially the Vedic one, the way both J. Krishnamurti and U.G. Krishnamurti would, in our times, avoid using the lingo of either the Hindu or the Buddhist enlightenment traditions.

The concern behind such an act could well be that when there is a radically new insight, it has to be kept bare and free, without being clothed in the language of the old, so that the new teaching is not perceived as a mere continuity of what has existed, although there may be certain philosophical links. To fail to see the difference and the freshness of approach is to be caught in the potholes of tradition.

Marking the difference between the approaches and methods of science and spirituality could be of interest here. If science always builds on the past, spirituality seeks the dissolution of the past. In science the theories are always interrelated; the new one cannot emerge without the presence of the existing one. Further, we have to make the new discovery a part of the scientific structure. This is essential, and science works by rejecting as well as building on previous theories. Hence the concept of progress is applicable to science, not to spirituality.

Spirituality works differently. At least with the Buddha, it was not a case of building on the past. When he came into the state of nirvana, it was not like building on what the Upanishadic seers had said or done before. It was, in fact, the other way round. You reject all that is there, all that has been said and done before; the old ways are eschewed. The dead past has to be wiped out for the new way to emerge. And yet, what a sage comes into—though in his own peculiar manner—is not an utterly new discovery but the *same* thing, in the sense that it is the same state of being that those who are ready, come into: it is a state where conflict has ended, where sorrow has ceased, where the binary mind has gone quiet. Indeed, it is the natural state of every human being.

The sage, given his distinctive background, gives expression to experience in his own unique way; some, like Ramana Maharshi, for instance, may use the already available traditional language and symbols to express themselves. However, the 'method' cannot be replicated and the 'message' cannot be made a part of the old structure. It has to be seen for what it is: a creative continuity while being a radical departure from what has existed, and this new way, over a period of time, may degenerate and fall into another rut and give rise to yet another radical departure.

EXPLORING DIFFERENT PATHS

The doctrine of ahimsa, non-violence, is central to Jainism. With ahimsa as its mahavrata, great vow, and in its stringent concern for avoiding harm or violence to all life forms, Jainism is unlike any other religion. On the surface there may be some similarities between Jainism and Buddhism, especially with regard to the doctrines of karma and rebirth, but that could be said of all Indian enlightenment traditions.

According to Jain philosophy/cosmology, everything in the world is produced by matter (pudgala), except soul (jiva) and space. Even karma is matter but in a subtle form. Samsara is nothing but ajiva, entanglement of jiva in matter.[8] The liberation of jiva from ajiva is moksha, which can be realized only by shedding karma by gradual means, and ultimately by absolute withdrawal from outward life. This could also result in sallekhana, fasting unto death. This absolute freedom from the bondage of karma is the state of 'being without form', the state of perfection pervaded by a passionless, ineffable peace. To the criticism that such a stringent practice of ahimsa or giving up all action is tantamount to suicide, the Jain would argue that it is better to mortify the flesh and kill oneself than to harm or kill any other living thing.

Gautama was evidently not drawn to Jainism, probably

the dominant religion at the time, although it must be said that in the last stage of his sadhana, he did practise the Jain kind of extreme asceticism, if only to discover its value and limitation and reject it as being counterproductive to the purpose of nirvana. However, in the beginning of his career, Gautama seemed to have found Sankhya philosophy quite congenial and had accepted Alara Kalama as his guru. Coming from Kapilavastu, probably named after Kapila, the founder of Sankhya, Gautama must have been familiar with at least some of its doctrines.

Scholars say that Sankhya philosophy was extra-Vedic, if not pre-Vedic. Whatever the case may have been, it has had a considerable influence on several schools of thought including Buddhism, and especially Patanjali's philosophy of yoga. Kapila, like the Upanishadic seers and the Buddha, rejected the need for divine aid, prayers, rituals and sacrifices as he felt they were counterproductive to freedom from suffering and self-realization. It is quite likely that the Buddha's 'four noble truths' were informed by Sankhya's threefold pain and deliverance from suffering: 'One, that from which we deliver ourselves is pain; two, deliverance is the cessation of pain; three, the cause of pain is want of discrimination between Prakriti and Purusha, which produces the continued union; four, the means of deliverance is discerning knowledge/wisdom.'[9]

According to Sankhya, the world or reality is made up of two types of entities: Prakriti (nature/matter) and Purusha (spirit/consciousness), in many ways analogous to the Jain principles of jiva and ajiva. Purusha is the spiritual principle of the universe: intelligent, quiet and passive, yet it is the one that makes Prakriti work.[10] The world, with both its physical and psychological features, is the manifestation of Prakriti. And Prakriti in its manifest form, that is, the world, is constituted of three gunas or types of qualities: sattva (illumination), rajas (activity and pain) and tamas (darkness and stillness). These three qualities together put up the play of life that binds and conceals Purusha. Interestingly, it is sattva (through sattvic urges) that facilitates the liberation of Purusha when the distinction between Prakriti and Purusha is realized.

Understandably, Gautama found this philosophy helpful, especially the idea that nature, while it binds and conceals the Absolute Spirit, also facilitates liberation. In such a scheme of things, even suffering has a redemptive role; in fact, it is suffering that builds up the yearning for freedom from suffering.

REJECTION OF ALL PATHS

Alara Kalama taught some form of yoga, which involved a discipline of the body-mind: pranayama, self-control; dhyana, meditation; and ekagrata, concentration of mind. Indeed, yoga, developed by Patanjali as a wholesome discipline and complete philosophy in the second century CE, was a vital component in a sramana's quest for freedom.

The practice of yoga, and meditation in particular, appears to have come easily to Gautama. It seems his body-mind had already been fine-tuned to take to meditation like a duck to water, for he could enter into samadhi, the higher states of consciousness, in a short period of time.

Gautama's guru Alara Kalama claimed to have attained the pure state of the *self* (Purusha), or what was called the state of 'nothingness' after several years of sadhana. So when Gautama said that he had entered this state after a brief period of sadhana, the guru could see that Gautama was already an advanced and gifted yogi, and he invited Gautama to be the leader of the sangha. Gautama declined the offer. He had not abandoned samsara to become the guru of a sangha but to find himself and to bring to an end the very cause of all suffering. He also realized that this goal had not yet been reached, despite his attainment of the so-called highest state. He was still not free of desires and conflicts, which meant that either he had failed to attain the real state of nothingness or that it really was not beyond the machinations of the mind.

Once this realization dawned upon him, Gautama left Alara Kalama and joined the group led by Uddaka Ramaputta, who claimed to have gone beyond the state of nothingness to come upon the real *self* or the state of 'neither-perception-nor-non-perception'. Gautama hoped that Uddaka would be able to lead him to that highest state of being. Again, in a short period of time, Gautama was able to enter the state of 'neither-perception-nor-non-perception', only to realize that this was not the state of absolute freedom either.

The spiritual path is not only 'sharp as the edge of a razor and hard to cross, difficult to tread', as the *Katha Upanishad* warns, but is fraught with a hundred deceptions as well. One has to be like the Upanishadic Satyakama, honest to the core, if one has to avoid going adrift on this difficult path. Transcendental states or mystical experiences, contrary to popular understanding, can be imprisoning rather than liberating. One may be deluded into thinking that a mystical experience is the highest state, the state of enlightenment.

This may well be illustrated with reference to U.G. Krishnamurti's life. During his sadhana, like Gautama, U.G. Krishnamurti could enter different planes of samadhi in a short period of time. Once, during a discussion on death by J. Krishnamurti, he actually underwent a near-death experience that altered his consciousness and his very perception of life. After such a tremendous life-altering experience, one might easily believe it to be the ultimate state of enlightenment when, in actuality, one may not be entirely free from the machinations of the mind. U.G. Krishnamurti was honest enough with himself to know that there was a radical shift in his consciousness all right, but he was not free yet, and so it could not be the state of enlightenment.

As he said, 'I practiced yoga, I practiced meditation, studied everything. I experienced every kind of experience that the traditions talked about including samadhi. Then I said to myself, "Thought can create *any* experience you want—bliss, beatitude, ecstasy, melting away into nothingness. So, this can't be the thing, because I'm the same person, mechanically doing these things. Meditations have no value for me. This is not leading me anywhere."'[11] It was this radical doubt and ruthless honesty that brought about the ultimate release from the stranglehold of the deceptive self.

Talking to Sariputra about his days with Alara Kalama and Uddaka Ramaputta, and his own experiences of nothingness and the state of 'neither-perception-nor-non-perception', the Buddha says:

I went to Alara Kalama. He was kind and he said to me, 'You may stay here, my friend. This doctrine is such that a wise person can soon enter and dwell in Dhamma, having realized it for himself through direct knowledge.'

It was not long before I quickly entered and dwelled in that Dhamma, having realized it for myself through direct knowledge.

But the thought occurred to me, 'This Dhamma leads not to disenchantment, to dispassion, to cessation, to stilling, to direct knowledge, to Awakening, nor to Unbinding, but only to reappearance in the dimension of nothingness.' So, dissatisfied with that Dhamma, I left.

In search of what might be skilful, seeking the unexcelled state of sublime peace, I went to Uddaka Ramaputta. It was not long before I quickly learned the doctrine and the discipline and could enter the state of neither-perception-nor-non-perception. But the thought occurred to me, 'This Dhamma leads not to stilling, to direct knowledge, to Awakening, but only to reappearance in the dimension of neither-perception-nor-non-perception. So, dissatisfied with that Dhamma, too, I left.'[12]

Thus, long before U.G Krishnamurti understood this, Gautama had realized that the experience of nothingness and the state of 'neither-perception-nor-non-perception' did not conduce to the absence of passion and tranquillity, and that it could not be the 'fourth state' or the state of nirvana. For he knew he was not free of the greedy self. There was no eternal *self*; instead, the sense of having come upon the eternal *self*, the so-called Purusha, had only been a projection of the mind, a delusion.

Years later, talking about Alara Kalama and Uddaka Ramaputta, the Buddha warns the monks of the deceptive nature of experiences, especially of mystical experiences to which many get attached, and advises them to 'surmount' such deceptions if they have to free themselves from the 'wheel of becoming'.

These mystical states are induced by the mind. The mind can create any state, any experience. Further, the mind strengthens itself through experience. All experiences, however profound or mystical, give life to the thinker, the self. Take the case of a drug like LSD. With such drugs, our sense of time and space is blurred, we feel expansive and lose the sense of separation. But once the effect wears off, we are back to what we were.

Similarly, mystical experiences don't touch or change the core of the self. At best, they can loosen the grip of the self, may even alter our perception of reality and our being, and the problems one had thought impossible to overcome may melt away, but the self never disappears.

Having realized this truth, it seems that Gautama needed to try out the extreme asceticism practised by yogis and Jain monks. Who knew, maybe rigorous tapas could burn up all the 'negative karma' that still lay buried in his being. Perhaps extreme tapas was the only means left now to excoriate the last traces of tanha, desire, still clinging to him like fine dust. Resolved thus, Gautama plunged into an extreme form of tapas. He sought total seclusion and denied himself even the basic needs of the body. For some days he lived on roots and fallen fruits and, if nothing else was available, survived on moss and grass. Eventually, he gave up eating altogether. He was desperate, like a drowning man, hoping against hope that this path would somehow help him stay afloat and get him to the other shore. But the result was a near disaster.

> My body became extremely emaciated. My limbs became like the jointed segments of bamboo stems ... My backside became like a camel's hoof ... My spine stood out like a string of beads ... ribs jutted out like the rafters of an old, run-down barn ... My scalp shrivelled and withered like a green bitter gourd ... The skin of my belly became so stuck to my spine that when I thought of touching my belly, I felt my spine as well ... If I tried to ease my body by rubbing my limbs with my hands, the hair fell from my body ... If I urinated or defecated, I fell over on my face right there ...[13]

This brings to mind U.G. Krishnamurti doing tapas in a cave in Rishikesh and trying to survive by eating grass. Or Allama

Prabhu, the twelfth-century sage, who probably went through a similar experience. Later, in one of his vachanas, prose poems, he warned that it was imperative to feed the body and keep it fit and healthy. J. Krishnamurti never failed to point out that one had to desist from doing things that would irrevocably damage the nervous system and weaken the body. And could it be the same kind of warning we hear in the following verses of the *Isha Upanishad*?

> To darkness are they doomed who worship only the body, and to greater darkness they who worship only the spirit.
>
> Worship of the body alone leads to one result, worship of the spirit leads to another. So have we heard from the wise.
>
> They who worship both the body and the spirit, by the body overcome death, and by the spirit achieve immortality.[14]

So there was a lesson to be learnt from this terrible experience. By starvation, Gautama had almost destroyed the body but not the self, for he seemed more conscious of himself than ever.[15] He had only succeeded in letting the body almost burn itself to death but had not managed to burn up the negative karma, let alone the self. So it was not the body that was the problem here but the mind, which seemed to use every trick under the sun to perpetuate itself. It was the mind that had to be starved of its sustaining power and immobilized. But how could that be done? Can the mind starve itself to death? Why would the mind destroy itself?

There is no time when the mind or the self is absent. Even in the so-called deep-sleep state, the self never ceases to be; it goes into a sort of hibernation, only to spring back into play once we are out of sleep. As U.G. Krishnamurti would say, 'It is a speculation on your part that you were not there during deep sleep. When you are not there after the deep sleep only then you can say you were not there in the deep sleep. If you were really not there during the sleep then you cannot be there now.'[16] It is misleading, therefore, to use the idea of deep sleep as an example or even as a metaphor, as classical Vedantins are accustomed to do, to talk about the self-less state.

Is there then no way out of this prison of the self?

Different spiritual traditions offer different solutions: do more yoga or meditation; practise tantra yoga; starve the body; deny yourself all forms of pleasure including sex; isolate yourself from society and avoid interactions with people; think that you are not the thinker or the doer, for only God is; reduce yourself to dust; pray and surrender to God wholly and absolutely; believe that 'thou art that', that you are Brahman; just let go of everything ...

There are methods and more methods, different upayas, techniques, and all of them seem to work up to a point; yet, the door remains locked and there is no other key. The structure of thought seems endless, like Indra's net, like millions of mirrors reflecting each other in never-ending patterns. It is tanha, craving after things, clinging to things, the constant process of trying to become something other than what you are, which can never be fulfilled. But the mind never gives up. If, on one hand, the restless mind seeks permanence in things that are transient, on the other, it desperately seeks a place to rest in, to be at peace, by way of projecting an eternal entity: God, Creator, Purusha, the Absolute Principle and so on. There is no way out within the structure of such a mind. Having said that, there is no other instrument or agency than the mind. This is the paradox!

The discovery that aham, ego, is a self-perpetuating substance and will never cease by itself, is a dead end. This is the core issue one has to come to terms with at some point in one's spiritual quest. The mind is the only instrument we have in order to probe, to delve deep within, even to reduce thought and try to reach a point of stillness by way of concentration on some object or by intense observation. But the self will not disappear, will not fall dead.

So the future Buddha was firm and still like the tree under which he lay. There was a flash of memory from the recent past. He remembered the moment he had spent under the roseapple tree close to the land that had been recently ploughed. The sight of the dead insects had put him in a strange, transcendental state of consciousness.[17] That state had come unbidden, like a sudden drizzle of rain from the heavens. There had been no effort; it had not been an act of will. It was as if the world, hitherto framed and constricted by thought, had broken open to a vast expanse of silence and peace.

But now, there was no way he could invite that state of equanimity, which was not pleasure, which had nothing to do with sensuality or with unskilful mental qualities, to come to him. He had experienced all that had to be experienced, all that the tradition proclaimed to be the highest state, but it had not ended his conflict. Self-mortification had not helped his situation either. There was no path he had not tried and all paths had been journeys in the wrong direction. Now it would be like sailing on an uncharted sea, with no compass and no clue as to where he was going.

Gautama was ready but the body, weak and emaciated, was unwilling. He had to start consuming food to regain his strength and begin his journey afresh. As if in answer to his prayers, from the nearby village came a young girl called Sujata, carrying a bowl of milk and rice to offer to the forest deity. She saw a man stretched out on a bed of dry leaves. Going closer and observing his tattered robes, covered in dirt and dust, she knew he was an ascetic gone weak without water and food.[18] She knelt down and, using her delicate fingers, fed him with drops of milk. It was amazing how his body imbibed the little drops of milk like parched earth sucking up the first raindrops, and he felt energy trickle into his limp and exhausted body.

From then on, Gautama fed himself regularly with little portions of food, regaining his strength. Then, according to the Pali canon, he went to Uruvela and, beside the Niranjana river, found 'an agreeable plot of land, a pleasant grove, a sparkling river with delightful and smooth banks, and nearby, a village whose inhabitants would feed him', and he decided that 'it was just the place to undertake the final effort that would bring him enlightenment'.[19]

Six years had passed since Gautama had left his family and Kapilavastu in search of truth. He had wandered the treacherous forests and led the harsh life of a sramana, and there was hardly any sadhana he had not put himself through. He had sat at the feet of two spiritual masters and found their teaching limited and even misleading. Despite the wonderful, at times terrific, mystical experiences he had undergone, and the extreme form of asceticism he had practised in order to break the chain of bondage, he had remained a captive of samsara. He had, of course, learnt much from his experiences and the lessons life had taught him, and realized many truths, but he was not yet free.

He was thirty-five years old and this quest could not go on for much longer. It had to end *now*, either in fulfilment or in death. Determined thus, Gautama sat under the Bodhi tree: 'My flesh may wither away and my blood may dry up until only skin, sinews and bones remain, but I will not give up ... until I have found liberation, I will sit here unflinching and utterly still.'[20]

Nirvana

When the future Buddha sat under the Bodhi tree (the 2,600-year-old tree is still in existence in a grove in Bodhgaya), it is difficult to know what exactly happened. The Pali canon states that Gautama looked deep into the heart of things, reflected upon the conditioned nature of life, progressively entered into the four jhanas or levels of samadhi and gained the insight that forever transformed him. This insight convinced him that he had been freed from bondage.

Therefore, is this the way Gautama became a Buddha? Here is the account of the process from the *Majjhima Nikaya*:

> Now when I had eaten solid food and regained my strength, then, quite secluded from sensual pleasures, secluded from unwholesome states, I entered upon and abided in the first jhana, but the pleasant feeling that arose in me did not invade my mind and remain.
>
> With the stilling of applied and sustained thought, I entered upon and abided in the second jhana … Then I entered upon and abided in the third jhana … Finally I entered upon

and abided in the fourth jhana ... But the pleasant feeling that arose in me did not invade my mind and remain.

When my mind was thus purified, bright, unblemished, rid of imperfection, I directed it to knowledge of the recollection of past lives. I recollected my manifold past lives, that is, one birth, two births ... a thousand, a hundred thousand births; many cycles of dissolution and evolution of the universe ...

This was the first true knowledge attained by me in the first watch of the night. Ignorance was dispelled and true knowledge arose, darkness was dispelled and light arose.

Then with the divine eye, which is purified and surpasses the human, I saw beings passing away and reappearing, inferior and superior, fair and ugly, fortunate and unfortunate, and I understood how beings pass on according to their actions.

When my mind was thus purified, bright, unblemished, rid of imperfection, I directed it to knowledge of the destruction of the taints. I directly knew as it actually is: 'This is suffering ...'; 'This is the origin of suffering ...'; 'This is the cessation of suffering ...'; 'This is the way leading to the cessation of suffering ...'; 'These are the taints ...'; 'This is the origin of the taints ...'; 'This is the cessation of the taints ...'; 'This is the way leading to the cessation of the taints.'

When I knew and saw thus, my mind was liberated from the taint of sensual desire, from the taint of being, and from the taint of ignorance. When it was liberated there came the awareness, 'It is liberated.' I directly knew, 'Birth is destroyed, the holy life has been lived, what had to be done has been done, there is no more coming to any state of being.'[1]

Almost all books on the Buddha base their telling of this event on the above passages from the Pali canon, literally interpreting it as an act of supreme, uncompromising *will* and the result of deep contemplation into the nature of existence.

Once, a seeker approached Sri Ramakrishna and said that he

had been yearning to see God for many years. Sri Ramakrishna led the man to a nearby river and held his head under water. A minute later he released the man from the water and asked, 'What were you feeling?' The man cried, 'What could I feel or think in such a terrible situation? I was panting for breath.' Then Sri Ramakrishna is believed to have said, 'If and when you yearn for God the way you gasped for a breath of air, you'll see God.'

There is no doubt that Gautama's firmness of mind, his determination to see the truth—even if he had to die in the process—was something like this great hunger Sri Ramakrishna spoke about. But this is only the first step. What ensues later remains something of a mystery because once a person enters nirvana, while he is aware that he has been liberated and that dukkha has ended, he will never be able to pinpoint and assert what it is that caused the liberation.

Now let us consider what Buddha is believed to have said. Though there are certain words and expressions within the given account that are quite problematic, there are also some clues that do indicate what might have occurred. *I directed it to knowledge of the recollection of past lives. I recollected my manifold past lives, that is, one birth, two births ... a thousand ...* This is a problematic statement. If taken literally, we will end up believing in the reincarnation theory, which goes against the very core of the Buddha's teaching. This subject will be taken up in the following chapters, so suffice it to suggest here that when the Buddha declares 'I directed it to knowledge of recollection of the past ... I saw beings passing away and reappearing ...' it could mean the birth and the dissolution of the self and the many streams of identities it creates and maintains, not the literal birth of an individual. So what the Buddha may have suggested is that in the state of awareness he gained, he could see the entire, relentless play of the self, its birth and its disappearance, its reappearance and final dissolution.

Now, the Buddha's choice of expressions to describe his 'mental' state, for instance, '… such feelings … did not invade my mind and remain … I knew directly … with the divine eye … I saw …' are interesting and quite revealing. Thinking is always in terms of the past and the future, and it leaves its traces behind. What the Buddha's choice of words may indicate is that his stepping out of the river of samsara and on to the shore of nirvana was an act of *seeing*, which has to be distinguished from verbal, dialectical, oppositional thinking. This act of 'seeing'—'*I knew directly*'—is of a different order, suggestive of immediacy and directness, totally different from what we call 'thinking'.

Generally, our idea of seeing is also thinking; what we see is always already a translation in terms of the past, of memory. We do not see things as they are; it is always an interpretation based on our perceptions, using language: soft, hard, good, bad, beautiful, ugly, freedom, bondage, samsara, liberation and so on. In short, there is no seeing without words, without interpretation. That is the nature of thought: to assess and judge in terms of the past or future, and this evaluation is always framed in terms of dualities.

In this context, what U.G. Krishnamurti says can help us appreciate the problem better. He says, 'Where is the seeing? What do you call seeing? Bringing back [memory] is not seeing. Seeing is ending … The seeing is the ending of what you say you are seeing. Outside and inside are the same, whether you say it to me or to yourself, and so long as that keeps happening, you cannot see. Seeing is the ending of that process—they are one and the same.[2]

What he is suggesting is that there is an act of seeing that is not in terms of words, in terms of the past or future, but an act where thought or language as we understand it is not in operation. And this act of *seeing* is also simultaneously an *action* in itself, bringing about the dissolution of the thought structure. If this is so, what the Buddha is reported to have said after attaining enlightenment —'I directly knew'—is in line with the act of 'seeing' described by U.G. Krishnamurti.

This is difficult to understand because, as with thinking, our listening too is already an interpretation in terms of our past. As mentioned earlier, this past prevents us from truly seeing. Perhaps this is the reason why sages talk about enlightenment, though rarely and reluctantly, by pointing out what it is *not*, for it falls in the realm of the unknown and the unknowable. In other words, depending upon the need, a sage may abstract that state of being and offer some clues, not as a nugget of knowledge for contemplation but as something to be seen then and there and done with.

Ultimately, nirvana is not something that can be known but something to be lived through. It is not an experience that can be transmitted or shared either. One has to discover this for oneself. So we have to stop *here*. The understanding is that all attempts at understanding nirvana are an exercise in self-defeat. This is self-knowledge in the sense that knowledge cannot dissolve the divided self, the self cannot find entry into *that* which is not of the self, into that which is vast, boundless.

THE MISSING LINKS

With the discovery of more and more of what are called transitional fossils, there are several theories on offer to explain the transition from animal, hominid or primate to Homo sapiens. But we cannot claim to know with any certainty how and when exactly this transition took place or what actually caused this great transition from apes to humans. This gap in our understanding of human evolution is generally referred to as the 'missing link'. Perhaps the best we can say about it is that the transition was triggered by a genetic mutation or maybe some innate potential already present in the animal manifested itself.

The Buddha's near-death experience under the roseapple tree had led him on to the death experience under the peepal tree. But, as said earlier, whilst we have some clues, we cannot say with any certainty what exactly transpired to cause this 'death'. The most we can say is that it certainly could not have been the result of an epistemological penetration, a product of discursive thinking or even of will. We do not know how and when precisely this radical shift or *seeing* takes place. This may be called the second or the other missing link in human evolution, in the sense that we do not know exactly what catapults a seeker into the state of unitary consciousness or nirvana.

What transforms a caterpillar into a butterfly? Some inner device or potential! Similarly, there seems to be some inbuilt device within the human which, when triggered, brings in its wake the death of the divided self and the birth of a new human being, now present in the undivided state of consciousness. However, we are not able to identify the cause that triggers this process of enlightenment, although most spiritual discourses are constructed on the assumption that we know the cause that can bring about enlightenment.

As already explained, nirvana cannot be brought about by an act of will or engineered or replicated through any method or sadhana whatsoever. At best, sadhana can prepare the ground for enlightenment but there is no guarantee that enlightenment *will* occur. The search cannot bring it on; only the end of search can, if at all. Of course, there has to be a search for it to be abandoned, the search that ceases with the realization that, finally, the very search is the barrier. It is the realization of the mind that it cannot solve the problem it has created in the first place.

> This atman is not attained by instruction
> or by intelligence or by learning.
> By him whom *it* chooses is the atman attained.
> To him the atman reveals his true being.[3]

You will have to replace the word 'atman' with 'nirvana' to get a sense of what is being suggested. Lest the notion of 'grace' be misunderstood, it is crucial to reiterate that nirvana is not something bestowed on a lucky person or handed over on a platter by some external agency or God. Perhaps, when all efforts cease, grace or the inner nature takes over and enables the *seeing* that finally brings to an end the continuity of the self.

As U. G. Krishnamurti would say, the search is a real thing, a tremendously serious thing, for you will know that 'all those to whom this kind of a thing [nirvana] has happened have really worked hard, touched rock bottom, staked everything'.[4] Indeed, you have to go the whole hog, as they say, go through the process wholly and honestly, finish with yourself totally, and you give up without knowing how to give up (since it is not an act of will), for 'grace' to descend upon you or, to put it more aptly, for that which is within you to open up.

The Buddha's attempts to attain nirvana through various methods makes it clear that enlightenment occurred only after giving up the various paths and spiritual techniques on offer. But this needn't be the case each time. With Ramana Maharshi, for instance, there was hardly any search or sadhana, and the period between his near-death experience and death experience was comparatively short. Nature intervenes in ways we do not know.

THE PROBLEM OF EVIL

Buddhist traditions and many Buddhist scholars often present the process of enlightenment as a heroic battle against Mara, the enemy or the tempter. This is a poetic description of the death pangs of the self but hardly does justice to the real thing. In Buddhism as well as in all the other enlightenment traditions of India, there is no notion of 'evil'. There is only error or a faulty perception of reality, which is due to ignorance; herein, the self is born. In other words, the self is the error, the ignorance.

An understanding of the notion of evil is in place here. The idea of evil is, of course, an ancient one. Evil as an independent power or principle, forever in battle against good, was probably first developed fully as a concept in Zoroastrianism. The story goes like this: When Creation was complete, everything was good and perfect, but Angra Mainyu, the Deceiver, the Evil One, entered into every particle. Hence Creation became a compound of good and evil, light and dark, wisdom and ignorance. And the human, who is a natural and integral part of creation, also became a compound of both good and evil.

Thus, the human is torn between good and evil. That is the conflict in every bosom and the imperfection in the world. If Creation has to become complete again, if good has to be recovered, evil has to be vanquished. Accordingly, it becomes the duty of man, in fact, the great purpose of man's very existence, to side with good, with light, and engage in the 'holy war' against evil. Joseph Campbell writes,

'It is supposed that with the birth of Zoroaster (variously placed between c. 1200 and c. 500 BC), twelve thousand years following the creation of the world, a decisive turn was given the conflict in favour of the good, and that when he returns, after another twelve millennia, in the person of the messiah Saoshyant, there will take place a final battle and cosmic conflagration, through which the principle of darkness and the lie will be undone. Whereafter, all will be light, there will be no further history, and the Kingdom of God (Ahura Mazda) will have been established in its pristine form forever.'[5]

Scholars may say it is difficult to trace with any certainty the origin of ideas such as good and evil, the idea of the ultimate victory of good over evil, the coming of the Kingdom of God and so on, and that they were already there in some embryonic form in earlier times, which Zoroastrianism developed later. Whatever the case may have been, the important thing is that these ideas were to be found in all ancient cultures, and all major religions were influenced by them. However, for our purpose, we understand that it was notably from Zoroastrianism that these ideas were later taken into Judaism and then Christianity (the evil one here being Satan) and Islam. All three religions more or less share the same cosmology.

Interestingly, the idea of evil as an independent principle never took root on Indian soil. The myth of Prajapati or Creation should offer the clue. It is the primordial God/entity itself that splits in two and becomes not only man and woman but all creation.[6] This is crucial to our understanding of the notion of enlightenment vis-à-vis the notion of salvation as found in the Semitic religions.

According to the Hindu cosmology, God, humans and the universe are not distinct and separate. All is One, tad ekam. The splitting of one into two, into male and female, life and death, is the beginning of the play, the lila of Brahman. In Buddhism, the origin of things is simply and neutrally referred to as the 'beginningless past' or 'root desire'. However, this play or root desire brings in its wake not only joy and wonder but also fear, sorrow, insecurity and lack, because of which there is also a deep yearning to return to the state of primordial unity, the state beyond joy and sorrow. In other words, one can go on with the samsaric play and taste of the joys and sorrows of life, but one would never know the 'peace that passeth understanding'. Therefore, if the human being has to be free of sorrow and the sense of incompleteness, and enter the state of enlightenment, one has to move beyond the play of dualism.

All major enlightenment traditions in India teach the same thing: desire and ignorance of our true nature are the causes of suffering and death; human beings are constitutively immortal and each person is always already God/Brahman/Buddha. The human is already divine in the sense that the energy or power that created the world (not that one can posit a beginning to creation) is the same energy that is operating in the human being and in all Creation.

But if man is made in the image of God, in the sense that Creation is distinct from or outside divinity (the orthodox Judeo-Christian interpretation, magnifying the difference to the extent of creating an unbridgeable gulf between the two, though it could be read differently), the goal of knowledge or the salvation of man would mean not to see or realize God, here and now in oneself and in all things, but to know the relation of God to His Creation and to surrender or 'link one's will back to that of the Creator'.[7]

There is no such covenant (between God and man) in the Indian enlightenment traditions. Man's separation from the primordial unity is seen not as a historical event or as a sin (to be redeemed) but as a *psychological* event, as the birth of aham, the self or the ego (rooted in fear and desire; alienated from the source), the dissolution of which constitutes enlightenment.

The self/ego has no separate existence; it is an illusion in the sense that in actuality the ego is neither independent nor separate from all things. To put it in a different perspective, in the words of Joseph Campbell, 'As long as an illusion of ego remains, the commensurate illusion of a separate deity also will be there; and vice versa, as long as the idea of a separate deity is cherished, an illusion of ego, related to it in love, fear, worship, exile, or atonement, will also be there.'[8]

MARA: THE FEAR OF DEATH

Mara is that movement of desire or fear in the form of the ego that creates an illusory sense of separation from all things. This is the first and last mystery that has to be penetrated and overcome to attain enlightenment. Mara was the last frontier Gautama had to cross to reach nirvana. The Buddhist tradition dramatizes this critical moment in the form of a battle against Mara and his forces (daughters), charmingly called Desire, Unrest and Pleasure. This Mara is not Angra Mainyu, Satan or some evil force outside of human consciousness. He is the 'enemy' within, one's own self as a barrier constricting the free expression of life and energy.

From within the perspective of the Hindu and Buddhist enlightenment traditions, we may even see, metaphorically, Mara's encounter with the future Buddha as the meeting between Yama, the Lord of Death, and Nachiketa, in a different time and space. In the *Chandogya Upanishad*, Nachiketa talks with Yama and seeks the knowledge of Brahman. In response, Yama says, 'Even the gods were once puzzled by this mystery. Subtle indeed is the truth regarding it, not easy to understand. Choose some other boon, O Nachiketa.' In an almost similar way, we see Mara offering Gautama the sovereignty of the whole world if he will renounce Buddhahood. Like Nachiketa, Gautama also rejects Mara's offer of pleasure and power over the world.

In Buddhism, as in all Indian enlightenment traditions, the ego is regarded as the movement of pleasure (not in the Freudian sense but in the sense of craving for or clinging to things, tanha). The ego is also what binds one to pleasure and pain, death and rebirth. It is this overcoming of the fear of death, of the pleasure movement coming to an end and the breaking of the chain of bondage, that the legend dramatizes in the form of a fierce battle between Gautama and Mara.

Sitting under the bodhi tree, Gautama remains silent and still against Mara's ravings, for any movement of thought in any direction only adds momentum to the self and strengthens it. *This* is the act of seeing. You cannot fight and win over the self, because combat is the stuff the self, Mara, is made of. But when there is no reaction, there is no space for the self to move and play around or wage battles. As a result, the self crumbles and burns itself up without a trace. That is the death pang of the self, the dissolution of fear, the seeing and awakening into a state of being where the egoistic mind, Mara, is no more the dictator, no more the centripetal and centrifugal force of the Buddha's consciousness.

Once this happens (*seeing*, which triggers *action*), once the ego gives way, the hitherto incarcerated energy within the body is released—an explosion of energy!—and the human being is transformed. Over seven days—seven night watches—Gautama is believed to have undergone radical changes before entering the state of nirvana. It is of crucial importance to note that upon coming into this state of nirvana, Gautama did not say 'I am liberated' but 'It is liberated'.

When I knew and saw thus, my mind was liberated from the taint of sensual desire, from the taint of being, and from the taint of ignorance. When it was liberated there came the awareness: 'It is liberated.' I directly knew: 'Birth is destroyed, the holy life has been lived, what had to be done has been done, there is no more coming to any state of being.[9]

The use of the pronoun 'it' indicates that Gautama, as a person, as an identity caught in the web of samsara, had disappeared. Life, the life energy that had been conditioned by culture, caught in the binary modes of thinking and living, of 'I' and 'thou', subject to joys and sorrows, good and evil, birth and death, was liberated. There is no 'other' in this state of being; all is one, with no boundaries or frontiers. And the individual becomes not divine or God but fully *human*.

The way U. G. Krishnamurti described his coming into the natural state is quite revealing and should attest to what the Buddha implied when he said 'It is liberated'.

How I got into this state I will never be able to tell. I may trace it back to a particular point and beyond that I don't know what happened. There is no story; my autobiography comes to an end. It is finished. It is just living.

The search has come to an end. The continuity of all kinds has come to an end. The evolution has come to an end. It is finished, complete. Everything is done by itself. It is just a flower giving out its own fragrance.[10]

THE MYSTIQUE OF NIRVANA

The word nirvana (Sanskrit), nibbana (Pali), literally means 'blowing out', 'extinction' or 'becoming extinguished', as when a flame is blown out or a fire burns out. Hence the term 'blowing out' has been generally used to refer to the extinction of desire/greed, hatred and ignorance/delusion.

According to Thich Nhat Hanh, the noted Vietnamese Buddhist monk and an important influence in the development of Western Buddhism,

> Nirvana is the extinction of all suffering. Our suffering comes from our wrong perceptions, our misunderstandings. The purpose of meditation is removing wrong perceptions from us. You have wrong perceptions of yourself and of the other and the other has wrong perceptions of himself and of you. This is the cause of fear, hatred and violence ... even ideas like being and non-being, birth and death, coming and going are wrong ideas. Ultimate reality is free from all of these ideas ... That is why nirvana is the removal of ideas that are the base of suffering.[11]

However, the notion of 'extinction' continues to pose problems for scholars, especially Western scholars. Volumes have been written to figure out what it could possibly mean.

The late Walpola Sri Rahula, a Sri Lankan Buddhist monk and a leading Buddhist scholar, wrote in *What the Buddha Taught* that most writings and even discourses by monks on nirvana only confused the issue rather than clarified it. 'The state of nirvana can never be explained completely and satisfactorily in words, because human language, used by people to express things and ideas experienced by their sense organs and their mind, is too poor to express the real nature of the Absolute Truth or Ultimate Reality.' But the 'ignorant people' get stuck in words like an elephant in the mud.

Nevertheless, as Rahula admitted in his seminal work, 'We cannot do without language. But if nirvana is to be expressed and explained in positive terms, we are likely immediately to grasp an idea associated with those terms, which may be quite the contrary.'[12]

It is a state of being that cannot be captured by words, which by their very nature fragment reality or frame reality as opposites, so nirvana is often described not in terms of what it is but in terms of what it is not. Therefore, the Buddha speaks of nirvana mostly in negative terms, such as that which is achanta, uninterrupted, akata, uncreated, nirodha, extinction, achutta, deathless, vimmutti, liberation, and so on.

Addressing Sariputra, the Buddha describes nirvana like this:

> Here, Sariputra, all dharmas are marked with emptiness, they are neither produced nor stopped, neither defiled nor immaculate, neither deficient nor complete. Therefore, Sariputra, where there is emptiness there is neither form, nor feeling, nor perception, nor impulse, nor consciousness; no eye, or ear, or nose, or tongue, or body, or mind; no form, nor sound, nor smell, nor taste, nor object of mind ... there is no ignorance, nor extinction of ignorance; there is no decay and death; there is no suffering, nor origination, nor path; there is no cognition, no attainment and no non-attainment.[13]

However, even these negative terms have been often misunderstood, avers Rahula.

> Because nirvana is thus expressed in negative terms, there are many who have got a wrong notion that it is negative and expresses self-annihilation. Nirvana is definitely no annihilation of self, because there is no self to annihilate. If at all, it is the annihilation of the illusion, of the false idea of self.[14]

I believe we need to review these interpretations and understand 'annihilation' differently. In a sense, nirvana does involve the annihilation or extinction of the self, that is, the annihilation of the self-protecting, self-perpetuating self, the ego. Thus, what actually gets annihilated is not the mind or factual memories but emotional memories. In effect, the self is purified of its 'taints'.

This can be better understood in relation to the notion of 'cooling'. This term suggests not a *complete* annihilation of the mind but only the fires of the ego, the human passions such as attachment and aversion, which are extinguished. That is to say, when Gautama attains enlightenment, he as a person, as an identity with a past, is reduced to just the bare facts cleansed of all emotional identification and content.

The Buddha says:

> The citta (consciousness) is in its original nature pure, but the manas (the mind, the self) and others are not, and by them various karmas (vasanas) are accumulated and those are the impurities (or defilements).
>
> On account of defilement from the beginningless past, the pure self ('true mind' or Buddha mind) is contaminated; it is like a soiled garment which can be cleansed.
>
> When the garment is unsoiled, or when gold is freed of its defects, they are restored and will not be destroyed; so it is with the self when remedied of its defects.[15]

The self now exists not as a master but as a servant. It exists as a 'burnt seed', no longer capable of reproducing or multiplying itself, and in that sense there is no rebirth for that 'self', no becoming. The five skandhas, senses, operate fully and purely without interference from the now powerless, toothless self.

Ramana Maharshi explained the mystery in this way:

> The jnani (the enlightened) continually enjoys uninterrupted, transcendental experience, keeping his inner attention always

on the source, in spite of the *apparent* [italics mine] existence of the ego, which the ignorant imagine to be real. This apparent ego is harmless; it is like the skeleton of a burnt rope—though it has form, it is of no use to tie anything with.[16]

Avoiding religious metaphors, almost in clinical terms, U. G. Krishnamurti said:

In the natural state the mind can never interfere, it is finished. The role of the mind as the dictator is over. It comes only at your bidding to supply factual memory, and when there is no use for it, it is gone. And there is silence, pure consciousness, consciousness without thought.[17]

This is *perfection*: the individual, freed from the stranglehold of the self, has become fully *human* and lives in communion with the cosmos. This is the Tathagata, the Perfect One, who has thus gone from the world of samsara. Yet, he is also the one who has arrived as a new human being with no self-consciousness because the frontiers have been dissolved.

When the Buddha declares that all dharmas are empty, what he is saying is that in the state of nirvana, since the ego is extinguished, the naming process has come to an end, which means no 'formation' is taking place. There is nothing defiled or incomplete because there is no duality. There is no feeling, no perception, no body, no form, no cognition, no birth nor death because identification is dissolved; the coordinator, the self or the interpreter does not come into play and so things are seen as they are. It is neither attainment nor non-attainment, in the sense that that state of pure consciousness or pure being is always already there; once the grip of the self is gone, *that* begins to express itself and you cannot put a name to it.

In short, kalpana, imagination, the foundation on which we have built our world, culture and identities, is knocked off.

The faculty of imagination is what distinguishes humans from animals. Unlike humans, animals live in their natural state, in a world that is real, not imagined. It is through imagination, conceptualization and applying categories of thought to the world around us, giving names and forms to our sense of being and doing things, that we have created samsara, the world we live in. It is not that without the mind the world will disappear or cease to exist. That world exists and it is what it is, like fire, forever in a state of flux and burning, but the mind cannot comprehend the totality of it.

So what is shaken off in the state of enlightenment is the imagined world and the imagined self or vikalpa, conceptual constructions. This is cittavimukti, liberation of the mind. All things imagined from time immemorial, all experiences and knowledge accumulated over millions of years of human existence, dissolve and then what is left is sarvakalpanavirahitam, pure consciousness without the touch of thought.

With imagination gone, such a state of being cannot be described as this, that or anything. We may understand this better in the light of what U.G. Krishnamurti says of the natural state. When he is looking at something, say a watch, a tree, a man or a woman, there is no operation of the memory in his consciousness. He does not tell himself that it is a watch, a tree, a man or a woman because there is no process of identification that occurs; neither is there any dialogue with the self. His consciousness remains in a state of emptiness; this is pure consciousness. But the moment somebody asks him a question about something, his prompt answer come from his past knowledge, from factual memory.

Translating sensory perceptions into images is the work of the imagination, the self, and this is the way the self operates and survives. We have an image of ourselves and, in relation to that image, we create images of others around us. All our relationships are transacted through these images. These images are the stuff of our emotional memories, our passions. A table is not just a table; it is always *my* table, *her* table, a *nice* table. And it is the same case with the people around us. They build up our egos, give us joy and sorrow, motivate us into action and help construct the world we live in.

In the state of enlightenment, this image-making process has come to an end because the image maker, the interpreter of sensory perceptions, has become silent. It is not that there are no thoughts in such a state of consciousness; they do come and go like a river in flow, but there are no embankments or boundaries, nobody there to interpret the stream of thought, for this wakeful state is empty of ideation.

In other words, there is no division in this state of consciousness. Since the individuated consciousness, the ego, is dissolved, since there are no frontiers to this state of consciousness, it is referred to as the 'void' or 'emptiness'. On the subject of 'emptiness', volumes have been written, but let us forget all the tedious, rather tortuous exegesis. Emptiness simply means that the interpreter has ceased to operate. We'll discuss this in depth in the chapter on Sunyata.

Sages are Human Flowers

Buddhism does not consider Siddhartha Gautama as the only 'Buddha' or enlightened one, nor does it view nirvana as an exclusive state of being or 'property' of a Buddha. It is not fixed in time and space, an exclusive or single historical event. Instead, it is a continuing process through human history even if, for a single human being, his personal 'history' comes to an end. Hence, the Buddha's coming upon nirvana is generally explained as a rediscovery, and his dharma, a re-proclamation. It is so because nirvana or the Buddhadhatu is a natural state, always already there.

Perhaps this is the way to understand the liberation of Jesus Christ and Prophet Muhammad as well, where these occurrences were not historically unparalleled or one-time events but a 'rediscovery', a return to the state of unitary consciousness. And, if one may suggest, Jesus and Prophet Muhammad's going away to the hills (for about forty days) and what happened to them there can be seen as a 'death experience', which is a precondition to liberation. This death, as explained earlier, is the breaking down of the binary self, essential before coming into the state of pure consciousness. Legends and scriptures clothe this event in mystical terms, for example, as a meeting with God or the Archangel.

Like the Buddha, Jesus Christ and Prophet Muhammad were enlightened masters. There is no need to compare and contrast or even integrate the way these sages lived and what they taught, although one may find several parallels in them. Just as a daffodil or rose gives out its own fragrance, every sage—a human flower, is unique and different in his expression although his essential message is always the same: to end sorrow and lead humanity out of its deeply entrenched sense of separation into the state of undivided consciousness.

BUDDHA NATURE

We are all manifestations of Buddha consciousness, Christ consciousness. This is not the historical Gautama Buddha or Jesus Christ in the sense it is understood in parochial terms; this is *life*, the fundamental state of every human being. This potential to be a Buddha or a Christ, that is, to be free of conflict and suffering, to transcend the divisive consciousness or samsara, is within every individual and the potential for this state is always present. Divinity is not an external state of being or an external agency. The name we give to that state of tranquillity is secondary.

The individual—every individual—is the question, the answer and the saviour. A sage can come from anywhere and at any time. A sage is he who has realized his potential, who has brought suffering to an end. These are human beings who bring home the wonder and mystery of life, indicating the possibility of ending sorrow, ending the thought structure, the self that is the cause of sorrow. It is in *this* sense that such sages are the saviours or 'messengers of God', not in the orthodox religious and exclusive sense of the term, fixed in time and space.

However, by putting them on a pedestal and worshipping them as gods, messiahs, avatars or bodhisattvas (in exclusive terms), we have misread their messages and created structures of belief and faith that have become the source of conflict, violence and sorrow. This is not going to help and it is not the way to consider these liberated beings. As explained above, their presence enables us to understand that there is a possibility of realizing that state of being. Instead, what we are doing is to imitate their lives and to create this imitation all over the world. And as a result, we create Buddhists, Hindus, Christians and Muslims and thereby give rise to division and conflict.

The Biology of Nirvana

In *Digha Nikaya*, a major Pali text, the mahapurusha lakshana or physical characteristics of the Buddha are described. We are told that the Buddha had an elongated body and long arms with a span equal to body length; his hands and fingers were long as well. On an oblong face, he had a protruding and well-formed nose and wide blue eyes. His sexual organs were concealed in a sheath. His body was golden in colour; his head was shaped like a turban with stylized lumps and so on. To these were later added another eighty secondary characteristics.

But of all these physical attributes, the stylized lumps on the head and long ears began to be depicted prominently in the images of the Buddha 500 years after his passing away, around the first century CE. Buddhist traditions attributed these marks entirely to good deeds done in former births and did not regard them as physical changes that could have come over Gautama on attaining nirvana. Around the second century CE, the Mahayanists, in particular the followers of the Vajrayana (Tantra) school of thought, spoke of the Buddha as the Dharmakaya, transmuted body, one who is in communion with the cosmos. This, however, still failed to throw any light on the recorded physical attributes of the Buddha.

Perhaps the prevalent attitude towards the body, in opposition to the mind or soul, was such that it was hard to conceive of liberation in physical or biological terms. For instance, 'This body is born and it has death,' declared the *Maitreya Upanishad*.

> It has originated from the impure secretions of the mother and father; it is the abode of joy and sorrow and it is impure ...
> It is built up of primary fluids, subject to grievous maladies, abode of sinful actions, transitory and diffused with agitated feelings ... It always naturally exudes at the appropriate time impure secretions through the nine apertures (eyes, ears, etc.) and smells foul ... It is associated with the mother in impurity at birth and is born with the impurity caused by childbirth ... Viewing the body as 'I' and mine is like smearing oneself with faeces and urine in the place of cosmetics ...[1]

In contrast to many such Hindu traditions, one may argue that Buddhism does not regard the body and mind as being two separate entities. There is no clear-cut division between the body and mind; rather, the belief is that the body and mind combine and interact in a complex way to constitute an individual. And in one's spiritual journey, only when the body is kept fit and healthy can it aid in the development of insight and wisdom.

Yet, when we dig deeper, we find that Buddhism is not entirely free from anti-body philosophy either. In certain Buddhist scriptures, the body is seen as a source of troublesome desire and, almost echoing the view of the body in the *Maitreya Upanishad*, is depicted as unwholesome and an object of disgust. Meditating on the loathsomeness of the body is considered to be a particularly powerful method for countering attachment to sensual pleasures. For instance, the canonical text, *Anguttara Nikaya*, warns:

> A boil, monks, is another word for this body composed of the four properties, born of mother and father, fed on rice and porridge, subject to inconstancy, rubbing and massaging, breaking-up and disintegrating. It has nine openings, nine un-lanced heads. Whatever would ooze out from it would be an uncleanliness oozing out, a stench oozing out, a disgust oozing out. Whatever would be discharged from it would be an uncleanliness discharging, a stench discharging, a disgust discharging. For that reason, you should become disenchanted with this body.[2]

The above quotations from both Hindu and Buddhist traditions should more or less sum up the then prevalent views against the poor body: an obstacle in the path of spirituality, a troublesome burden and foe to be vanquished in order to attain enlightenment. Kundalini yoga and tantra yoga offered a radically different understanding of the body, both as a field of energy and as a channel of divine power, even though they were regarded as esoteric disciplines and therefore of no value to ordinary religious seekers and laymen. Once the kundalini energies are activated, they transform the body-mind and catapult the human into the state of nirvana. Hence it is disappointing that despite the prevalence of such disciplines, Buddhism failed to carry and convey in its discourses the critical role the body played in the radical transformation of an individual.

It is not as if there have been absolutely no attempts in the past to remedy this defective view, but all these attempts have been subsumed under spiritual discourses that were and are predominantly framed in psychological terms. Thanks to the biological sciences today, we have a better and more holistic understanding of the body-mind. Importantly, the reports of the experiences of Pandit Gopi Krishna, the Mother (of Puducherry) and U.G. Krishnamurti can now throw some new light on this most enigmatic subject and offer vital clues in understanding the biological basis of enlightenment.

PANDIT GOPI KRISHNA AND KUNDALINI POWER

Born in a Kashmiri Pandit family in 1903, Gopi Krishna led the life of an ordinary middle-class man. After seventeen years of regular meditation and sadhana, at the age of thirty-seven, he experienced the first stirrings of kundalini power. It was something he had least expected and it came upon him like a tidal wave at sea.

> Suddenly, with a roar like that of a waterfall, I felt a stream of liquid light entering my brain through the spinal cord. Entirely unprepared for such a development, I was completely taken by surprise, but regaining self-control instantaneously, I remained sitting in the same posture, keeping my mind on the point of concentration. The illumination grew brighter and brighter, the roaring louder. I experienced a rocking sensation and then felt myself slipping out of my body, entirely enveloped in a halo of light.... I was now all consciousness, without any outline, without any idea of a corporeal appendage, without any feeling or sensation coming from the senses, immersed in a sea of light simultaneously conscious without any barrier or material obstruction.[3]

It was only the beginning of an incredible journey into an uncharted sea, for he had no clue what was happening to him. The sadhus and mystics he met and the scriptures he consulted could not offer him a convincing explanation either. And the experience was not one of absolute peace and ecstasy; instead, it was often terrifying and torturous.

The few brief intervals of mental elation—the typical expansion of his consciousness, a radiant current flowing through his body—were followed by fits of depression so acute that he had to muster all his strength and willpower to keep himself from succumbing to their influence. Repeatedly, he felt he was dying and his body burned as if the scorching sun had risen inside his body.

Gopi Krishna had to endure pain and the other side effects of the physiological changes taking place within his body for fifteen years before the state of 'cosmic consciousness' stabilized. Then, given his sceptical bent of mind, he took another twenty years before he went public about the radical transformation he had undergone.

It was a case of radical transformation in the microbiology of every cell, tissue and fibre of the organism. The arousal of kundalini implied the activity of a hitherto sleeping force, and the start of 'a new activity in the whole system to adapt it to a new pattern of consciousness by changing the composition of the bio-energy or subtle life force permeating the whole body'.[4] The terrible discomfort he had to endure was due to the process of purgation, the internal purification of the organs and nerves; it was kundalini shakti 'hammering and pounding them into a certain shape'. It was a terrific journey that put him in a state of higher consciousness, yet he never equated himself with sages like the Buddha or Ramana Maharshi.

Gopi Krishna said,

'I do not claim to be illuminated in the sense we ascribe illumination to Buddha ... I am still very much entrenched in the world and have not completely risen above it. I feel more at home in calling myself a normal human being, like millions of others who inhabit the earth.

All I claim is that for more than forty years, I have been undergoing a most extraordinary experience which is now a constant source of wonder and joy to me ... I am always conscious of a luminous glow, not only in my interior but pervading the whole field of my vision during the hours of my wakefulness ... In other words, I have gained a new power of perception that was not present before. The luminosity does not end with my waking time. It persists even in my dreams ... In every state of being—eating, drinking, talking, working, laughing, grieving, walking or sleeping—I always dwell in a rapturous world of light.[5]

Gopi Krishna was an extraordinarily honest mystic the likes of which are hard to find today. Perhaps the kundalini was not fully awakened in him, but he was definitely a living example of the liberating powers of kundalini, of the cellular revolution within the body that lifts one out of that which is limited, the 'I' consciousness. And he never tired of reiterating that it is false and delusional to think that 'the human mind can win entry to supersensory realms without affecting the body in any way'. Sadly, even the advocates of kundalini yoga, he pointed out, 'failed to give the corporeal frame the status it deserved as the sole channel for achieving a transcendent state in yoga practice'.[6]

He died in 1984 at the age of eighty-one after a severe lung disease. Until then, he worked tirelessly to correct the false perception of the body and to persuade scientists to investigate the phenomenon. He believed such research would ultimately lead to the discovery of the biological basis of enlightenment and it could, in the course of time, also put an end to the rivalry between science and religion and the needless controversies and conflicts among the various religions.

THE MOTHER AND THE CELLULAR REVOLUTION

In the 1960s, around the time Pandit Gopi Krishna was still in the throes of the revolutionary changes in his body-mind and was trying to figure out the nature of these changes, the Mother underwent what she called 'cellular changes' in her body, which brought about a radical shift in her consciousness and in her very understanding of spirituality.

The Mother, or Mirra Alfassa as she was earlier called, was born in Paris on 21 February 1878. At a young age she became an accomplished artist, pianist and writer. However, her primary interest was spiritual development. In 1914, she came to Puducherry (then Pondicherry) and met with Sri Aurobindo. Two years later, renouncing all her old affiliations and activities, she joined Sri Aurobindo in his experiments in Integral Yoga.

After Sri Aurobindo's passing away in 1950, till her death on 17 November 1973, she carried on the work she had started along with him, with unexpected but revealing discoveries. The reports of her experiences and the tremendous physical changes she underwent offer an account of the biological foundation of enlightenment.

In 1962, after what seemed like a brief illness, she began to sense signs of her body undergoing biological mutation: '... a sort of decentralization ... as if the cells were being scattered by a centrifugal force ...' She would feel terribly weak at times, yet, something, untouched, was fully conscious of what was happening ... 'witnessing everything ... like matter looking at itself in a whole new way'.[7]

Taste, smell, vision, touch, sound—the sensory perceptions began to undergo a complete change. Now and then she experienced bursts of energy that caused pain. At times she would feel that she was dying, that she was going to explode.

The sensation was not what religious people assumed to be joy or bliss, she asserted, but a sense of alarm, fear, anxiety, pain. She said, '... it's really and truly terrifying ... it's truly a journey into nothing ... You are blindfolded, you know nothing.'

It was the body that was involved in the process, not the mind. There was a struggle within the cells between the old habits and something new that was trying to emerge. In other words, it was the struggle of the body to cleanse itself of the *habit* developed over thousands of years of 'separate existence on account of ego.' Now it had to learn to continue without the ego, '... according to another, unknown law, a law still incomprehensible for the body. It is not a will, it's ... a way of being ...' and she felt that the body was everywhere. 'I am talking here about the cells of the body, but the same applies to external events, even world events. It's even remarkable in the case of earthquakes, volcanic eruptions, etc., it would seem that the entire earth is like the body.'

Everything is interconnected. The sense of separation is complete falsehood. The mind divides everything up. But here, in the body, the Mother asserted, everything is one. She pointed out:

> The speck of dust you wipe off the table, or ecstatic contemplation, it's all the same ... It's not a product of thought or imagination ... Dreaming, meditating, soaring into higher consciousness is all very well, but that seems so poor in comparison, so poor, so limited ... In the mental world, you think before doing the thing; here it's not that way ... No more memory, no more habits ... it's all spontaneous ... it comes, it comes in facts, in actions, in movements.'

'Salvation is physical,' she declared. The 'I' or the individual had no role to play in this process. It was the body with its innate intelligence *taking over and doing what had to be done.* She wondered why the spiritual teachers of the past sought liberation by abandoning their body, and why they had to talk of nirvana as something outside the body? 'The body is a very, very simple thing,' said the Mother. 'It does not need to "seek" anything. Why men never knew of this from the start. Why did they go after all sorts of things—religions, gods, and all those … sorts of things?'[8]

Once, talking about these 'cellular changes', she was to tell Satprem, her close associate, that the physical is capable of receiving the superior light, the truth, and of manifesting it. 'It is not easy, it requires endurance and will come when it will be totally natural. The door has just—just been opened—that's all; now we must go ahead.'[9]

U.G. KRISHNAMURTI AND THE NATURAL STATE

Sri Aurobindo did not live long enough to complete his spiritual experiments and actualize the 'supramental' manifestation, and the task was passed on to the Mother. But she died before the cellular changes were brought to fruition and could find their full expression. The burden of completing the process, it seems, was passed on to U.G. Krishnamurti. Many may find such a reading strange and even problematic. It was certainly not something like passing on the baton in a relay race!

However, whether such a reading makes sense or not, the fact remains that, in 1967, five years before the Mother's death, U.G. Krishnamurti walked through that 'just been opened door' to undergo a full-scale biological mutation and come into the natural state.

Born on 9 July 1918 in Masulipatnam, a town in coastal Andhra Pradesh, U.G. Krishnamurti grew up in a peculiar milieu of both theosophy and Hindu religious beliefs and practices. Exposed to such knowledge at quite an early age, he developed into a passionate and rebellious character but with a strong spiritual streak in him.

It was while pursuing his BA (Hons) course in philosophy and psychology at Madras University that U.G. Krishnamurti's spiritual search gained momentum. During this three-year degree course, he spent the summer in the Himalayas studying yoga and practising meditation. At that time, he came upon certain mystical experiences. Yet, deep within him, he realized there was no transformation. It seemed he had meditated and performed penance to no avail, for he was still deeply conflicted and also found himself burning with anger all the time.

He quit university. He had decided that he wanted to attain the state of enlightenment, and nothing less would do. One day, at his friend's suggestion, he went to meet Ramana Maharshi and asked him, 'Is there anything like moksha? Can you give it to me?' The sage said, 'I can give it, but can you take it?' The counter question struck U.G. Krishnamurti like a thunderbolt. He realized that nobody could 'give' that state to him; he had to find his own truth.

The next few years of his life were a roller coaster of sorts. In 1943, at the age of twenty-five, he married and started to work for the Theosophical Society in Madras (now Chennai). He also travelled extensively in India and Europe, giving talks on theosophy. The period between 1953 and 1964 was a time of great changes in him and the beginning of the metamorphosis he would undergo in 1967. In brief, he went to the US to get medical treatment for his polio-stricken son; he took up lecturing to earn a living; and he broke away from his family. After that, he began to drift aimlessly in London, a dry leaf blown hither and thither.

It was during this period that he underwent a near-death experience that altered his perception of life and eventually led him to his spiritual awakening. On 13 August 1967, on the completion of his forty-ninth year, the biological changes began to manifest. For the next seven days, seven bewildering changes took place and catapulted him into what he called the 'natural state'.

In seven days, the whole chemistry of his body, including the five senses, was transformed. His skin turned soft, and when he rubbed any part of his body with his palm, it produced a sort of ash. His eyes stopped blinking and his senses started functioning at the peak of their sensitivity. He developed a female breast on his left side. And the hitherto dormant ductless glands such as the thymus, pituitary and pineal, referred to as chakras in kundalini yoga, were reactivated. On the eighth day, he 'died'.

According to U.G. Krishnamurti, this was a 'clinical' death. He felt a tremendous burst of energy coursing through him, and all these energies seemed to draw themselves to a focal point in his body. He stretched himself on his bed and got ready to embrace death. Then a point arrived where the whole thing looked as if the aperture of a camera was trying to close itself, but there was something trying to keep it open, refusing to die. Perhaps it was the 'I', the residue of 'thought' (the fear of death, the fear of the unknown or the void, dramatized as Mara in Buddhist literature). After a while, there was no 'will' to do anything, not even to prevent the aperture closing itself. And it closed.

This process of dying, as U.G. Krishnamurti explained, 'lasted for about forty-eight minutes'. His hands and feet turned cold, the body became stiff, the heartbeat slowed down and he started gasping for breath. He was seized by death pangs. All thoughts, all experiences undergone by humanity from primordial times, whether good or bad, blissful or miserable, mystical or commonplace—the whole 'collective consciousness'—were flushed out of his system. He died on the eighth day only to be reborn in the state of 'undivided consciousness', untouched by thought. It was a most profound journey and a sudden great leap into the state of 'primordial awareness without primitivism'.[10] This was a cellular revolution, a full-scale biological mutation; it was the birth of the individual in the 'natural state'. This was a term he chose, preferring it over the term 'enlightenment'.

From then on, for nearly forty years till his death, U.G. Krishnamurti travelled the world. Wherever he stayed, people came to see him and to listen to his 'anti-teaching'. He talked openly of the natural state and responded to people's queries, answering their questions candidly, 'revealing all the secrets'.[11]

U.G. Krishnamurti often insisted that whatever transformation he had gone through was within the structure of the human body and not in the mind at all. Avoiding religious terms, he described the natural state as a pure and simple physical and physiological state of being. And he never tired of pointing out that 'this is the way *you*, stripped of the machinations of thought, are also functioning'.[12]

RAMANA MAHARSHI AND THE SAHAJA STHITI

There are several indications to believe that Ramana Maharshi also underwent physical changes, though he never described the state he had come into in explicitly biological terms.

Born as Venkataraman Iyer, on 30 December 1879 in Tamil Nadu, Ramana Maharshi grew up as a normal child with no apparent signs of future greatness. But on 17 July 1896, when he was about seventeen, he underwent a near-death experience and his life changed forever. In his words:

I was sitting alone in a room on the first floor of my uncle's house. On that day there was nothing wrong with my health, but a sudden violent fear of death overtook me ... I just felt I was going to die and began thinking what to do about it. It did not occur to me to consult a doctor or any elders or friends ...

The shock of the fear of death drove my mind inwards and I said to myself mentally, without actually framing the words: 'Now death has come; what does it mean? What is it that is dying? This body dies.' And I lay with my limbs stretched out still as though *rigor mortis* has set in ... I held my breath and kept my lips tightly closed so that no sound could escape, and that neither the word 'I' nor any word could be uttered. 'Well then,' I said to myself, 'this body is dead. It will be carried stiff to the burning ground and there burnt and reduced to ashes. But with the death of the body, am I dead? Is the body I? It is silent and inert, but I feel the full force of my personality and even the voice of I within me, apart from it.'

All this was not dull thought; it flashed through me vividly as living truths which I perceived *directly* [italics mine] almost without thought process. I was something real, the only real thing about my present state, and all the conscious activity connected with the body was centered on that I. From that moment onwards, the 'I' or Self focused attention on itself by a powerful fascination. Fear of death vanished once and for all.[13]

After this event, Ramana Maharshi lost interest in studies, friends and relations. One day, he just decided to leave home and go to Arunachalam. There, he would undergo series of death experiences and enter the sahaja sthiti, the natural state or the state of jivanmukta, one who has attained freedom while living.

The first death experience occurred six weeks after reaching Arunachalam, in the Patala-lingam, an underground vault in the temple complex, where he spent days absorbed in such deep samadhi that he was unaware of the bites of vermin and pests. The second experience took place when he was thirty-two. In his words:

> The landscape in front of me disappeared as a bright white curtain was drawn across my vision. I sat down near the rock ... My head was swimming and my circulation and breathing stopped. The skin turned a livid blue. It was the regular death hue and it got darker and darker.
>
> ... This state continued for some ten or fifteen minutes. Then a shock passed suddenly through the body and circulation revived with enormous force, and breathing also, and the body perspired from every pore. The colour of life reappeared on the skin. I then opened my eyes and got up and said, 'Let's go.' We reached Virupaksha Cave without further trouble.[14]

During his stay in the Skandasramam cave, where he lived from 1916 to 1922, Ramana Maharshi was to slip into samadhi a few more times. One way of understanding samadhi is that it is a state of being where the interference of the mind is completely obliterated, and the body takes over and transforms itself. Another way of understanding samadhi is that it is the body's way of renewing itself. During this time the stream of thought is cut; the person passes out and the body goes through 'death'. As U.G. Krishnamurti said, 'This "conking out" gives a total renewal of the senses, glands and nervous system: after it they function at the peak of their sensitivity.'

However, without getting into any polemics over this issue, the point that has to be highlighted and reiterated here is that Ramana Maharshi did undergo a biological mutation. By the time he came down and settled at the foot of the Arunachalam hill, where the ashram is located today, all the necessary changes within him had occurred. His discourse on the 'spiritual heart' as the seat of the Divine highlights these probable physical transformations.

The spiritual heart, he would say, is different from the muscular cavity that propels blood. Countless times he is believed to have said with great emphasis that the heart 'is the seat of consciousness or the consciousness itself,' located 'two digits to the right from the centre of the chest'. Sometimes, he would also refer to the heart as the seat of the atman or Brahman. Distinguishing the heart from the mind or the ego—which is the root of duality and creates the illusion of separation—he would point out the spot on his chest as the place where the *oneness* was felt. As he put it, 'This perception of division between the seer and the object that is seen, is situated in the mind. For those remaining in the Heart, the seer becomes one with the sight.'[15]

Disciples and admirers took the sage's words in good faith, although they had no clue as to what he actually meant. Yet, the idea of locating God, Brahman or the Self in a particular spot in the body may have confused and confounded many. Now, in the light of what U.G. Krishnamurti has said about the natural state of being, we could argue that Ramana Maharshi was possibly referring to the reactivated thymus gland.

After U.G. Krishnamurti underwent the physical transformations, he was to ascertain that the swellings that appeared on his body now and then were due to the reactivation of the ductless glands.

These glands are what the Hindus call chakras. These ductless glands are located in exactly the same spots where the Hindus speculated the chakras are. There is one gland here (slightly to the right of the midpoint of the chest), which is called the thymus gland. That is very active when you are a child, and so children have feelings, extraordinary feelings. But when you reach the age of puberty it becomes dormant—that's what the doctors say. When again this kind of a thing happens, when you are reborn again, that gland is automatically activated, so all the feelings are there. Feelings are not thoughts, not emotions; you feel for somebody. If somebody hurts himself there, that hurt is felt here—not as a pain, but there is a feeling. All feelings, not emotions like love and hate, anger or kindness, as we understand, are felt in the region where the thymus is located. That is where the physical, not emotional, oneness is felt or experienced.[16]

Unlike U.G. Krishnamurti, Ramana Maharshi may not have spoken of his state in explicitly physical and physiological terms, but he did speak a good deal about nadis, energy channels, as the natural energy of Atman-Brahman, which suggests, in unequivocal terms, the biological foundation of moksha. And when he said, 'The macrocosom is in its entirety in the body. The body is in its entirety in the heart. Therefore heart is the summarized form of the macrocosm,' he came closest to describing the sahaja sthiti in physical and physiological terms.

Surely such physical transformations must have happened to more people over the centuries. But why such changes should happen only to a few and not to many remains a puzzle. However, what is important to understand is that such a revolutionary transformation is possible. The lives of the sages who embody such changes indicate that the potential to be reborn as, or evolve into, a complete, compassionate human in a state of unitary consciousnes *does* exist.

BUDDHA NATURE: DHARMAKAYA

According to the Pali canon, the Tathagata is 'Dharmakaya', the transmuted body or the 'embodiment of truth'.

In the Nyingma tradition of Tibetan Buddhism, dharmakaya is symbolized by a naked, sky-coloured male and female Buddha in kamamudra, union. They are called Samantabhadra and Samantabhadri, and their form bears resemblance to the androgynous ardhanarishwara in Hinduism.

According to the Trikaya doctrine, developed in the first century BCE, dharmakaya constitutes the unmanifested, inconceivable aspect of a Buddha—also sometimes called 'tathagatagarbha'. It is out of this state of being or source that the Buddhas, and indeed all dharmas, phenomena, arise; and it is to this state they return after their dissolution. Some schools of Buddhism, however, consider this an essentialist view and not true to the Buddha's teaching.

Nonetheless, almost all Buddhist traditions agree that dharmakaya, the body of the Buddha, is marked by the mahapurusha lakshana, the thirty-two major signs. As discussed earlier, these signs indicate the physical transformations the Buddha underwent, especially the soft skin, radiant body, long ears like lotus petals and head shaped like a turban with stylized lumps.[17]

Corroborative evidence for this could be found in the physical transformations U.G. Krishnamurti underwent after he came into the natural state. During this process, his skin turned soft and radiant, he grew long ears like lotus petals, his sexual organ shrank and the glands in his head swelled, much like the stylized lumps we see in popular images of the Buddha. These glandular swellings were indicative of the tremendous 'pressure' building up in the body due to the explosion of energy and the biological transformations taking place. Once these transformations reached completion and the body settled in its new state, the swellings disappeared.

Since these changes—especially the long ears and cranial

protrusions—were conspicuous, and considered the physical signs of an enlightened being, these signs became a permanent feature in the depiction of the Buddha in Buddhist iconography.

There are other physical transformations that may not be noticeable by the physical eye but do occur. All of these transformations burn up or purify the self, and set it in its natural state. Along with these changes, the natural abilities of the body, what U.G. Krishnamurti calls the innate 'powers' or 'instincts' of the body, and what the Buddhist texts refer to as 'dhamma-cakkhu' and 'yatha-bhutam', are duly manifested.

Consider the following expressions used to describe the Buddha's state, found in most Buddhist texts.

'The dustless and stainless Eye of Truth has arisen.'

'Thus with right wisdom he sees as it is.'

'The eye was born, the knowledge was born, wisdom was born, science was born, light was born.'[18]

The terms 'dhamma-cakkhu', eye of truth, and 'yatha-bhutam', seeing things as they are, are interpreted and used rather idealistically by many teachers and practitioners of Buddhist meditation. It is claimed that a meditator will eventually develop the abilities of yathabhutam and dhamma-cakkhu. It is doubtful if meditation and sadhana can open up the 'eye of truth' or enable one to see things as they are, for they are not psychological attributes or mental skills and powers you can develop. Instead, they are the *physical* attributes of Dharmakaya, of one who has undergone biological mutation and lives in the state of nirvana. The canonical texts do not offer such a reading of dhamma-cakkhu. This could be because they had no understanding of the role the glands such as the thymus, pituitary and pineal play in the transmutation of the body-mind.

This needs explication. Ordinarily, we live in the 'unnatural' state, in the world of ideas. We see not with our eyes, experience not with our senses; we see and experience with our mind, through thought. We don't live the life of the senses because the mind is always manipulating the senses in terms of likes and dislikes. Hence there is already selectivity in our perception and experience of the world. There have been enough experiments over the years now to show that 'we look at the world through a tiny slit, and this narrow window on reality is even further restricted by censorship taking place between the eye and the brain'.[19] It is the mind that censures and censors the sensory data. In other words, the self is the interpreter interpreting the world. As long as this interpreter is in operation, there cannot be pure experience or pure perception of the world.

Only one who has undergone the physical or biological changes and has attained enlightenment can see, hear, taste and feel things as they are because the mind has been completely transformed. Now, the senses work independently and perceive the world as it is, without the interference of the self or the mind. This is pure perception.

As U.G. Krishnamurti says,

The eyes see things as they are; there is no differentiation, no comparison, no naming and all that. It is the mind that indulges in comparison, calling something more beautiful, someone more handsome or intelligent and all that … The eyes take in completely the 100 per cent of what is there. They say the eye cuts off 98 per cent and takes in only 2 per cent, but here, since there is no choice of any kind, the eyes take in the whole thing … This is not a mental state. This is not an experience at all. *It is not beyond the mind; it is just not of the mind.* The senses function that way, moment to moment and there is no interpreter there. This is a physiological phenomenon and so it is physically impossible for me to live in any other way except from moment to moment.'[20]

U.G. Krishnamurti never used Hindu or Buddhist terms to describe the faculties of the body in the natural state. Instead, he demystified and 'depsychologized' nirvana and described it in simple physical, physiological terms. However, there is no doubt that when he said 'the eyes see things as they are' or 'the eyes take in completely the 100 per cent of what is there', he was, in fact, referring to what the Buddha called dhamma-cakkhu and yatha-bhutam.

Consider this statement: 'Within this fathom-long sentient body itself, I postulate the world, the arising of the world, the cessation of the world, and the path leading to the cessation of the world.'[21] In the light of what U.G. Krishnamurti has said, the arising of the world or the self, suffering and the cessation of the self are all within the *body*. The self is a squatter; it uses the body and the five senses for its own continuity. Over the centuries, it has superimposed itself on every nerve end, every cell of the body. Therefore, if dukkha has to end, if the human being has to truly begin to function as a human, the 'I', with all its fears and anxieties, its sense of lack and insecurities and the animal trait of aggression, has to go. The senses have to be freed from bhava or bhavachakra, the grip of the self. Cleansing has to take place not just in the brain but in every cell of the body.

COMPASSION

It is said that Gautama renounced his family life and kingship and went in search of truth so he could find a way to end humanity's suffering, and it was compassion that made him share his insights with people. As a matter of fact, one who is in the state of nirvana cannot be but compassionate. But this compassion is not an act of will or a choice made as against, say, hard-heartedness; it is not the opposite of unkindness. It is actually non-volitional; it is the way a being who is enlightened lives and moves in the world. That is how life, freed from ignorance and duality, operates spontaneously and naturally.

Compassion is central to the notion of the bodhisattva and has a physical basis. Compassion is not 'karuna', which means kindness, but 'anukampa'. Anukampa is not affection or love; it is not even kindness. It means to 'tremble with'; more appropriately, it means to 'suffer with'. This meaning may come close to 'maitri' (Sanskrit) or 'metta' (Pali). In English, we would use the word 'empathy'. However, anukampa is not a mental trait but a physical and physiological response. It is the movement of life that is always right and manifests itself when thought is inactive or absent.

In other words, anukampa is related to the reactivation of the ductless glands, especially the thymus gland. Doctors say that the thymus gland is active in children until puberty, and it is what enables children to have extraordinary feelings. But, contrary to the medical theory, the thymus gland does not become entirely dormant or inactive after puberty. While in the case of a sage the gland is reactivated fully and it is what enables a sage to feel oneness with the world, in an ordinary human being it may be partially active. And this is what probably enables one to feel empathy.

There is the seed of compassion in acts of kindness. If we observe closely, we will know that when we have tender feelings for another or reach out to someone in a sorrowful plight, these feelings in us come with the slowing down of the mind or the thought process; there is a spontaneous quality to it. It could be the *thymus* pushing itself up and pushing us into such selfless acts. All existence is one. Compassion is an expression of that oneness, of that organic connection between all that exists. This connection is ruptured by the self.

Talking about this organic connection and drawing examples from experiments conducted on the behaviour of plants and trees, Lyall Watson, a noted biologist, shows that when a plant is maltreated, plants and trees close to the injured one 'empathize' with the 'victim'.

When a plant is deliberately abused or injured, it quickly produces tannin—its chemical defences against danger—and moves these into the leaves. While this is happening, other plants and trees around that plant go into this protective and sympathetic mode within minutes. For instance, when a hook thorn was deliberately thrashed, it was found that not only did another hook thorn about 2 metres away showed a 42 per cent increase in tannin but even a silver oak about 3 metres away produced 14 per cent tannin within an hour. There was no 'root contact' between them, yet somehow they had communicated.

What is more revealing and touching is to know that when an animal is injured or killed, other animals nearby and even plants and trees 'shake or tremble' in empathy. These revelations should lead us, says Watson, to a careful reappraisal of some hoary old prejudices, particularly the one that draws a hard and fast line between the plant and animal kingdoms and completely denies plants access to any of the abilities we reserve for the so-called 'higher' species. Watson suggests, 'There is good reason to presume, at least as a working assumption, that some kind of *awareness* is part of the experience of all living things.'[22]

Therefore, these revelations should enable us to move away not merely intellectually but more deeply, from individual, linear and analytical processes to more holistic and intuitive ways of seeing and experiencing the world. The neuroscientist V.S. Ramachandran believes that this 'linear thinking seems to be our default mode of thinking about the world', while 'nature is full of non-linear phenomena'. Extending the discussion in neurological terms, he speaks of a special class of cells called 'mirror neurons' that allow human beings to empathize with others. He illustrates the point by discussing a patient named Smith undergoing neurosurgery at the University of Toronto.

As is done usually during the surgery, Smith's scalp is perfused with a local anaesthetic and his skull opened. The surgeon places an electrode in Smith's anterior cingulate, a region near the front of the brain where many of the neurons respond to pain. Predictably, the doctor is able to find a neuron that becomes active whenever Smith's hand is poked with a needle. But what astonishes the doctor is that the same neuron fires just as vigorously when Smith watches another patient's hand being poked with a needle. Ramachandran writes, 'It is as if the neuron is empathizing with another person. A stranger's pain becomes Smith's pain, almost literally.

'Indian and Buddhist mystics assert that there is no essential difference between self and other, and that true enlightenment comes from compassion that dissolves this barrier. I used to think this was just well-intentioned mumbo-jumbo, but here is a neuron that doesn't know the difference between self and other. Are our brains uniquely hard-wired for empathy and compassion?'[23]

It is not just the brain but the whole body that is hard-wired for empathy, the basis of which probably lies in our ductless glands. Further, it is not just the brain and the body that are hard-wired; all life forms, in fact, the whole universe is a living web, a pulsating *body* of which human beings form an integral part.

BOOK TWO

Prajna-Paramita

The Perfection of Wisdom

The First Sermon

Our identities, our relationships and every single one of our experiences are informed and shaped by our ideas. 'All that we are,' declares the Dhammapada, 'is the result of what we have thought: it is founded on our thoughts, it is made up of our thoughts.' Further, all these thoughts, feelings and experiences belong to the past. We access them and process them, identify ourselves with them and call them our own but, in actuality, they don't solely belong to us. To presume that they are ours alone, and to cling to them and even seek their permanency, is an illusion and the cause of suffering.

The world and the self, even the body, are mere constructs. We construct ourselves as this, that and the other, and keep the process going lest it break down and reduce us to nothing, for somewhere deep within us we seem to know that it is not real, not permanent, and we are afraid. It is the fear of 'nothing', the fear of losing the known, the fear that we are, in actuality, not what we think we are or that we do not exist in the sense we think we exist as separate entities, is what keeps us marching on blindly. In the process, we succeed only by reaping sorrow. We are moving in the wrong direction.

In such a way of life, there is no freedom from conflict and suffering. It may sound hopeless and terrible, but that is the truth. Now, how would one teach such a thing to people? How would one tell people who are immersed in sorrowful samsara that there are only thoughts, no thinker; there is action but no agent; and there is nothing permanent! How would one make people see that their suffering is mind-made? It is a flaw in the mind's perception of reality, always seeing things as opposites: joy and sorrow, good and evil, life and death and so on. It is this *defect* in perception that needs to be corrected if we have to overcome conflict and suffering. After his enlightenment, the Buddha was confronted with this dilemma.

> Then, monks, I thought, 'Now I have gained the truth, profound, hard to perceive, hard to know, tranquil, transcendent, beyond the sphere of reasoning, subtle. For humankind, intent on its attachments and taking delight and pleasure in them, it is hard to see this principle: conditionings, the cessation of all conditionings and compound things, the renunciation of all clinging, the extinction of craving, absence of passion, nirvana.'[1]

On seeing the Buddha's reluctance to teach, the legend says that Lord Brahma pleaded with him. 'Lord, you must kindly preach the Dhamma. Look down at the human race, which is drowning in sorrow and waiting to be delivered. What you have come upon and seen is difficult to teach and hard to know, but there are some who will understand.'[2]

Hence, the compassionate Buddha gazed upon the world, decided 'to beat the drum of the deathless Nibbana' and set the Wheel of Dhamma in motion. The Buddha's teaching made possible a radical leap in human consciousness and gave that much-needed decisive turn to the enlightenment traditions the world over. His teaching was in some ways an extension and amplification of the Upanishadic insights but, more importantly, it marked a radical departure from the Upanishadic method and some parts of its doctrine, especially the atmavada.

Therefore, it would be incorrect and a case of oversimplification to state—as some Hindu swamis are wont to do—that Buddhism is a mere extension of Upanishadic teaching. On the contrary, it might be argued that it was the teachings of the Buddha and the subsequent Madhyamika philosophy that set in motion thought processes resulting in the development of many schools of thought, including Advaita Vedanta.[3]

Unlike the Upanishadic seers, the Buddha took the open road and shared his insights with anyone who was ready to listen and inquire, irrespective of caste, creed and gender. You could say that in true democratic spirit, he initiated what may be called a jnana yagna, and he held back nothing. During his last days, reflecting upon his life as a wandering sage, he tells Ananda, 'I have preached the truth without making any distinction between exoteric and esoteric doctrines, for, in respect of the truths, Ananda, the Tathagata has no such thing as the closed fist of a teacher who keeps something back.'[4]

THE NOBLE TRUTHS

The legend holds that after his enlightenment, the Buddha passed through Varanasi on his way to the deer park on the outskirts of Isipatana (presently modern Saranath). There he met with the five bhikkhus, his former companions during the time of his ascetic practice. Weeks back, on seeing him giving up the practice and consume food, they had left him in disgust, thinking he had reverted to a life of comfort and self-indulgence.

Now, when they see him approaching them, they are quite alarmed but decide to ignore him since they feel he has betrayed their cause. However, when the Buddha gets closer, the bhikkhus see a radiant glow emanating from his body and a compassionate smile on his face. They forget themselves and run forward to greet him. Before long we find the bhikkhus sitting at the feet of the Buddha, eager and ready to receive his teaching. And the Buddha speaks thus:

> Monks, there are two extremes: A life given to pleasures, which is sensual and unskilful. And a life given to mortifications, which is painful and unskilful. By avoiding these two extremes, monks, the Tathagata has gained the knowledge of the Middle Way, which leads to insight, to wisdom, to nirvana.
>
> What, monks, is this Middle Way?
>
> It is the Noble Eightfold Path, namely: right views, right intent, right speech, right conduct, right means of livelihood, right endeavour, right mindfulness, right meditation.
>
> The Noble Truth of Dukkha is this: Birth is suffering; aging is suffering; sickness is suffering; lamentation, pain, grief and despair are suffering; association with the unpleasant is suffering; dissociation from the pleasant is suffering; not to get what one wants is suffering; in brief, the five aggregates of attachment are suffering.
>
> The Noble Truth of the origin of Dukkha is this: It is this thirst (craving) for sense-pleasures, thirst for existence and becoming, which produces sorrow.
>
> The Noble Truth of the Cessation of Dukkha is this: It is the complete cessation of that very thirst, detaching oneself from it, giving it up, emancipating oneself from it.[5]

The Pali texts have arranged the first sermon in such a way that the essence of the Buddha's teaching is covered brilliantly in his very first talk to the five bhikkhus, even though the Buddha could never have preached in the form that we find today. This is doubtless the work of the canonical scribes. Nevertheless, even in this traditional, conflated representation, what is most interesting to note is that the Buddha begins with a feeling and an experience rather than an idea. He makes the fact of pain and suffering the basis of his teaching. He does not talk of God, good and evil, the meaning and purpose of life; nor does he promise salvation.

There is suffering and there is an end to suffering because he knows it is possible, because he *has* found freedom from suffering. Further, there are no good and evil actions; there are skilful actions that lead one to the path of liberation and unskilful actions that bind one to a life of suffering.

Is there a god? Is there a meaning and purpose to life? Is there a life beyond death? Well, once you end suffering, you will find the answers. Or the questions will have become irrelevant. You will know.

THE FIRE SERMON

After his first sermon at Isipatana, we are told that the Buddha went to Uruvela and then to Gaya; there, at Elephant Rock, he delivered the famous Fire Sermon.

One evening, while the Buddha and his disciples were sitting on the rock, they saw a vast flame rise from the hill opposite. The forest was on fire. It was an awe-inspiring spectacle and the Buddha saw in it an image embodying a deep, symbolic truth. He addressed the bhikkhus.

Bhikkhus, all is burning. And what is the 'all' that is burning?

The eye is burning, the ear is burning, the nose is burning ... the tongue is burning ... the body is burning ... the mind is burning ... forms are burning. Burning with what? Burning with the fire of greed, of hate, of delusion. It is burning with sorrow, with lamentation, with pain, with grief, with despair.

On knowing this, O Bhikkhus, one who is wise becomes weary of the eye, weary of the knowledge of the visible, weary of the feeling which arises from contact of the visible, be it pain, be it pleasure, be it neither pleasure nor pain....

When one is freed of all this, passion [attachment and aversion] fades out. With the fading of passion, one is liberated. When liberated, there is awareness that one is liberated. Birth is exhausted, the holy life has been lived out, what can be done is done, of this there is no more beyond.[6]

The Buddha uses this brilliant and fiery metaphor to speak of human living and of the nature of the human mind in particular. What is it that is burning, and what is it burning with? The body-mind is burning with the three fires of greed, hatred and delusion. In short, it is the self that is burning and exhausting itself. As long as the human burns with these fires, he continues to live in the unnatural state of becoming and sorrow, and cannot reach the coolness of nirvana.

The thinking process or thoughts are like noise that goes on and on, like the vibrations in the electromagnetic field; the thought, the noise, never stops. The fire is the *suffering*, the constant manipulation of the body and its senses towards achieving illusory goals. Having said that, once this noisy self is put in its place, the movement of thought or the vibration does not cease; only, its fire or 'passion' as the Buddha calls it, is extinguished.

Now, paradoxical as it may sound, the mind continues to

exist albeit in a different, transformed way: it does not indulge any longer in the translation of its thoughts. There are no likes and dislikes and no goals to be achieved because there is no seeker and no translator. In this state, the body takes over and begins to live in a rhythm natural to it and that is the 'calm, the coolness' of nirvana, and 'of this there is no more beyond'.[7]

WAS THE BUDDHA A 'PESSIMIST'?

With no theology, metaphysics or magic, nor any need for rituals or sacraments, this straightforward teaching may appeal to many but not to everyone. This is because the Buddha does not speak of concepts like God and Love, Beauty and Order. He only speaks of dukkha. So it is assumed that he is a pessimist, a nihilist and an agnostic. Any attempt to tackle these charges (set in a Western philosophical framework) will land us in fruitless binary arguments that will not serve the purpose of this narrative.

However, we have to admit that the *traditional* representation of the Buddha and his teaching can become problematic, especially because of its overemphasis on suffering and the pathologically persistent reference to disease, old age and death. Take the following sentence from *Buddhacharita*: 'How can anyone laugh who knows of old age, disease and death?' This sounds like a sad song, if not a persistent wail, that runs through many Buddhist texts. Life *can* seem very negative, for instance, when perceived by the so-called gurus of 'love' and their followers, who believe in the 'positive' approach to life!

Would a Buddha, one who has ended suffering, speak like a melancholic poet? Would he constantly throw the fact of suffering at people to draw them to the path?

Imagine the Buddha laughing at our assumptions and then answering our questions in this way:

'Sir, what is the cause of sorrow?'

'Non-fulfilment of desire is the cause of sorrow.'

'What then is the cause of joy?'

'Ah, the fulfilment of desire.'

That is how the Buddha may have actually presented things, but somewhere along the line things got twisted out of context and the Buddha was shown as being obsessed with thoughts of the misery of birth, old age and death. It seems the compilers of the texts projected their own fears, anxieties and longings on to the Buddha.

Joy and sorrow are facets of our everyday existence. Children are a joy to parents and they also cause pain and vice versa. Love offers great pleasure, joy and the sense of security we all feel we need. But when love is absent or denied, life can be very depressing. Laughter and tears follow each other, like the tail follows the monkey. So the Buddha couldn't have everlastingly talked only of suffering.

He may have said this: 'Listen, living is a compound of joy and sorrow, pleasure and pain, birth and death. But, remember, you cannot opt for one and reject the other; they are like two sides of the same coin. However, there is a state of being where all is one, where there is neither suffering nor joy. This is the state of tranquillity. Now go and live your life, enjoy yourself and try living mindfully and honestly. The day you feel tired of it all and are ready to find out what this is all about, you may return and we'll talk some more.'

Indeed, the focal point of his talk would certainly have been the fact of dukkha and the way to end it. In many ways, this approach may be compared with that of J. Krishnamurti. For about forty long years, he went around the world talking tirelessly about the problem of living, of jealousy, hatred, conflict and violence, what the Buddha called dukkha.

Apparently, on the stage from where he gave his talks, J. Krishnamurti always appeared deadly serious and his approach seemed negative. But we know how he drew people into a serious and critical reflection on the human condition and how he strove to set people on the path of self-inquiry, the goal being to free themselves from suffering. He was not one without a sense of humour, but it never came into play in his talks. His public image, therefore, was that of a severe, grim-faced teacher—for which, of course, he himself was partly responsible. In his normal one-on-one interactions with people, he joked a lot and laughed heartily. We know this from the writings of his friends who were witness to the jovial and witty side of his personality.

The Buddha's case must have been the same, but unfortunately the Pali canon has ignored the 'jovial' side of the Buddha and painted him as a grave and unsmiling teacher. Free of dukkha, a Buddha is one who lives and moves in harmony with the world, and he is like a child: innocent, unselfconscious and given to laughter and playfulness. Hence the 'laughing Buddha' had to be invented to make up for the loss!

THE NATURE OF DUKKHA

Once your awareness goes up a few notches, you know the human condition is dukkha, not only at times of calamity or during personal loss or sickness but even in normal conditions. Dukkha is much more than just sorrow and suffering. It is like a wound that affects our deepest nerves.

Dukkha is the search for permanence because nothing is permanent, because everything is in flux; dukkha is also wanting or desiring because there is no fulfilment, desire being a bottomless vessel; dukkha is the craving or clinging to things and people and ideas, because we are forever afraid of losing what we have. We are also afraid of the unknown.

Happiness is also dukkha, for in the very experiencing of happiness, love or pleasure is the fear of losing it. In fact, as strange and even dubious as it may sound, there is only fear at the bottom of every experience and it takes different forms: likes and dislikes, joy and sorrow, the search for security, knowledge, power and truth. Fear is the offspring of duality, separation; it *is* the self. If there is no separation, there is no samsara, no search and no experience, and hence no fear at all.

In Pali texts containing the Buddha's discourses, various kinds of happiness are included in dukkha. Even the pure spiritual states such as dhyana, supposedly free from even a shadow of suffering, are included in dukkha. 'In one of the suttas of the *Majjhima Nikaya*,' writes Walpola Sri Rahula, 'after praising the spiritual happiness of these dhyanas, the Buddha says that they are "impermanent, dukkha, and subject to change" (anicca dukkha viparnamadhamma). Notice that the word dukkha is explicitly used. It is dukkha, not because there is "suffering" in ordinary sense of the word, but because "whatever is impermanent is dukkha—yadaniccam tam dukkham".'[8]

This is so because even in the 'highest' state where there may be an alteration in the sense of time and space, in the very perception of reality, the self is nevertheless still in operation and, therefore, the 'becoming' has not ended. No wonder, therefore, that U.G. Krishnamurti should reject such spiritual states as 'thought-induced' states. Indeed, he often reiterated that in any and every experience, whether it is the so-called experience of God or bliss or just simple pleasure, the observer is still there, the self is very much in operation. In the natural state, however, there is no experience at all because the self, the experiencing structure, is absent.

Somewhere along the line, the primordial unitary consciousness ruptured and the human experienced separation from nature, from the totality of life. There are scientific theories to explain how and why this separation occurred, why—putting it in the language of science—hominids transitioned to Homo sapiens. It could have taken place due to some genetic mutation, as a self-protective measure and so on. And there are fascinating myths of creation in all cultures that attempt to narrate this separation in the human, though obviously this is not the case with other life forms.

Whatever the origin of this separation that marks the birth of the self, the 'I' consciousness, it also marks the beginning of lack, the sense of incompleteness and fear in the human heart. And our constant striving is geared towards filling that gap and overcoming the emptiness and fear, and it is a bottomless pit. It can never be filled up, and this is dukkha. It is like a wound that never heals, and it has penetrated into the very marrow of our bones, into every cell. Hence, U.G. Krishnamurti insists that it is a neurological problem. It is in that sense, perhaps, that we need to interpret Adam, Eve and the Fall, which is the primordial error; it is the ignorance of our oneness. To bring about this realization and enable our return to the state of the primordial unitary consciousness is the function of religion.

The word 'religion' is derived from the Latin word *religio*, which means 'to link back, to bind', to return to the source, to our natural state. But, over the centuries, religion has come to mean and function as a system of faith, based on the belief in and the worshipping of God. Related to it are moral principles or 'commandments' laid down in order to realize a specified (religious) goal. The Indian notion of Dharma, derived from the root 'dhr', to hold up, support or sustain, is sometimes used to mean religion, but it is not same as religion; rather, the concept of Dharma is quite complex, signifying many things. It is, in fact, the notion of yoga (though a clichéd, much abused term today), derived from the verb 'yuj', to yoke or bind together, that comes close to the Latin *religio*.

In Buddhism, this return to the primordial unity could be interpreted as nirvana, which is the state of the Buddha or Buddhadhatu. This is the natural state. This is Freedom. And this is possible. If the release from dukkha and return to the natural state is not possible, all our inquiry and search will be futile and absurd, and we will be stuck in the mire of sorrow forever. So the Buddha says:

> O bhikkhus, there is the unborn, ungrown, and unconditioned. Were there not the unborn, ungrown, and unconditioned, there would be no escape for the born, grown, and conditioned. Since there is the unborn, ungrown, and unconditioned, so there is escape for the born, grown, and conditioned.[9]

The real task of religion, therefore, is to end dukkha, to join us back with *that* which is 'unborn', 'unconditioned', to enable our return to the source and to become fully human. The cessation of dukkha is possible. This is a priori, for we know it is possible to end dukkha, otherwise we wouldn't be asking questions, searching for answers.

Indeed, it is dukkha that drives us up the path of pleasure, but the path of pleasure is what it is: a temporary escape from dukkha by way of seeking power, wealth, fame, love and sex, a substitute for the real thing, reaping in the bargain frustration, greed, envy, hatred, hurt and violence, which are but other forms of the same dukkha.

Yet, it is dukkha that sets up the inquiry, the search, as well, and that is the beginning of philosophy, of the religious quest. Dukkha or the deep dissatisfaction in us may also be a result of the impact of all those saints and sages on human consciousness, which is trying to burst out all the time, pushing us on to the path of spirituality so that the self is dissolved and dukkha comes to an end. In effect, it is the natural state within us that is pushing itself up, pressing us to seek the end of dukkha.

Is There a Middle Path?

The Middle Path suggests that both self-mortification and self-indulgence are not skilful ways of sadhana, for both extremities could irreversibly damage the sensitivity of the body-mind and strengthen the ego of an individual.

> Monks, these two extremes ought not to be practiced by one who has gone forth from the household life. What are the two? There is addiction to indulgence of sense-pleasures, which is unworthy and unprofitable; and there is addiction to self-mortification, which is painful, unworthy and unprofitable.
>
> Avoiding both these extremes, the Tathagata has realized the Middle Path; it gives vision, gives knowledge, and leads to calm, to insight, to enlightenment and to nirvana.[1]

But this wise counsel may begin to sound like middle-class morality: don't indulge in extremities of any kind, strike a balance, play safe and take good care of yourself! It may not appeal to many a spiritual seeker who wants to explore and experiment and find things out for herself. To think that you should strike a balance and follow a middle path in your spiritual journey may be a compromise, and that is not the best way to do spirituality.

You simply have to do what you have to do, and what is to be done will be different for each person. After all, that is what the Buddha himself did (remember the last phase of his sadhana when he almost starved himself to death), although the Pali canon finally has the Buddha endorse the Middle Path and claim that he could attain nirvana by scrupulously following this path and the noble eightfold path in particular.

However, philosophically, the Middle Path is a significant viewpoint and has far-reaching epistemological and ethical implications. As T.R.V. Murti argues, it is neither a neutral nor a 'third position lying midway between the two extremes, but a no-position that supersedes them both'.[2] It simply means we cannot assert that something is, or isn't, with any certainty. This path avoids absolute positions or the one-sidedness of perspective that takes any polarity as objective reality.

So, steering clear of eternalism (sasvatavada or the belief in atman) and nihilism (ucchedavada or the denial of continuity), rejecting both the affirmative and the negative views, the Madhyamikas maintained that there simply is no duality; there is only advaya, unity. This view is derived from their philosophical position that all things have dependent origination (pratitya-samutpada) and, therefore, all things are empty.

Now, before we discuss the notions of pratitya-samutpada and sunyata, it is imperative that we first consider the question of morality and the related noble eightfold path.

CAN MORALITY CHANGE PEOPLE?

The solemn promise to engage in or refrain from a certain thought or action in order to achieve a specified goal has never worked. To be specific, religious morality or moral teaching, or even the 'secular' ethical principles (shaped by political ideologies, which in turn were derived from religious moral vision) have been unsuccessful in achieving their intended goals. If they had succeeded, the world would not have been what it is today.

Morality may control human nature to some extent and for sometime, but it can never change it. Moral principles can curb 'negative' tendencies and push people to behave in a certain way. It is an age-old psycho-social engineering technique based on the assumption that man is basically 'bad' (not the other way around as is generally assumed), but with the hope that he will learn to be 'good', over a period of time under certain conditions.

In this context, if religious morality put a 'policeman' inside a man to monitor his behaviour, politics placed the policeman and the law outside to control and monitor society, but both techniques haven't been able to prevent crime and violence, let alone transform man and society.

In point of fact, this very attempt to control or regulate human behaviour and create a single model or ideal for all people has created such terribly complex problems and conditioned our minds to such an extent that we are no longer sure if there is a way out, or if there could be another way of living, where individuals are free of fear and violence that plague our societies today. Raging against such a morality, Nietzsche said:

> Almost every morality which has so far been taught, revered, and preached, turns against the instincts of life: it is condemnation of these instincts, now secret, now outspoken and impudent. When it says, 'God looks at the heart,' it says 'No' to both the lowest and the highest desires of life, and

posits God as the enemy of life. The saint in whom God delights is the ideal eunuch. Life has come to an end where the 'kingdom of God' begins.[3]

Nietzsche, of course, is talking of the Judeo-Christian morality, not about Indian ethical philosophy or Buddhist ethics, which are different. We will come to that soon. However, what Nietzsche says makes sense since morality as an *ideology* is geared towards, as said earlier, the psycho-social engineering of man and society, and when that is absolutized, it wreaks havoc. In that sense, God, that is to say 'morality', is the enemy of life.

There are no absolute moral truths. The ideas of right and wrong, good and evil are social constructs, not some cosmic principles in war with each other according to some divine plan or order. The so-called evil or adharma is born of the womb of the so-called good or dharma. Or is it the other way around? Whatever may be the case, what we need to critically examine is not what we consider to be bad, wrong or evil, but our very notions of good, right and divine, for therein lies the mischief.

Fear is a potent and toxic force and it is at the back of every form of morality. The fear of God and the fear of punishment may work as a deterrent for some people and for a period of time, but it cannot touch the core of a human being. So, ironical as it may sound, morality (the 'covenant' or 'promise' as it is called) exists in our lives more in a breach of the 'contract' than in reality—it couldn't have been otherwise. It's just that we have now invented new vocabularies to justify the killing. If we do not kill for selfish reasons, we kill for selfless reasons, for the cause of some ideology or god. The killing never stops. As Koestler would say, 'No historian would deny that the part played by crimes committed for personal motives is very small compared to the vast populations slaughtered in unselfish loyalty to a jealous god, king, country, or political system,' or what Koestler otherwise would call 'transpersonal ideals'.

The flaw, if any, is in human nature: 'Some potentially fatal engineering error built into the native equipment—more specifically, into the circuits of our nervous system—which would account for the streak of paranoia running through our history.'[4] Indeed, it is a neurological problem, as U.G. Krishnamurti would assert. In a nutshell, the flaw or error lies in the self: in our divisive consciousness, in our binary thinking, in the mind.

BUDDHIST ETHICS OR THE EIGHTFOLD PATH

Can the eightfold path be the way that could lead us out of this divided, sorrowful existence and into the waters of oneness and happiness? Buddhist traditions have put words in the Buddha's mouth to the effect that the Buddha achieved the breakthrough and attained nirvana by following the eightfold path. Is it only to give credence to the path and seek conversion, or is there something more to it?

The Buddha, while wandering in Kosala, entered Kesaputta, a town where the Kalamas lived. The Kalamas had heard that Gautama was an enlightened person. They went to him and paid homage. Then one of them asked the Buddha:

> 'There are some monks and Brahmins, venerable sir, who visit Kesaputta. They expound and explain only their own doctrines; the doctrines of others they despise, revile, and pull to pieces. Venerable sir, there is doubt, there is uncertainty in us concerning them.'
>
> 'Of course, under such circumstances it is only natural to be uncertain and in doubt, Kalamas. When there are reasons for doubt, uncertainty is born.'

'But, venerable sir, which of these reverend monks and Brahmins spoke the truth and which falsehood?'

'What do you think, Kalamas? Does greed, hate and delusion appear in a man for his benefit or harm?'

'For his harm, venerable sir.'

'That is being unskilful, Kalamas, to live in greed, hate and delusion. Such a man takes life, steals, commits adultery, and tells lies; he prompts another too, to do likewise.'

'Yes, venerable sir.'

'What do you think, Kalamas? Does absence of greed, hate and delusion appear in a man for his benefit or harm?'

'For his benefit, venerable sir.'

'That is being skilful, Kalamas, not to give in to greed, hate and delusion. Such a man does not take life, does not steal, does not commit adultery, and does not tell lies; he prompts another too, to do likewise.'

'Yes, venerable sir.'

'Listen, Kalamas. Do not believe something just because it has been passed along and retold for many generations, because it has become a traditional practice, because it is well-known everywhere, or it is common opinion, because it is what the scriptures say, because it sounds logical, because it accords with your philosophy, because the speaker seems trustworthy.

'But when you know for yourselves these things are unskilful, these things when performed and undertaken conduce to ruin and sorrow, then reject them.

'When you know for yourselves these things are skilful, when performed and undertaken conduce to well-being and happiness then live and act accordingly.'[5]

Kusala, which means skilful or helpful, and akusala, unskilful or unhelpful, are the key words in Buddha's ethical teaching. Words like 'good', 'bad', 'moral', 'immoral', 'shameful' and 'wicked' are judgemental terms that betray prejudice, intolerance and a lack of awareness. There are no moral judgement or commandments in Buddhist ethics. Commandments don't work; they only produce their opposites. That way, modern culture may be seen as an act of revenge against the old, religious morality. Every single commandment, whether religious or secular, has been twisted and turned upside down.

So what is kusala? We cultivate friendliness, kindness and truthfulness because they are skilful states, because they are helpful to free ourselves from hatred, spite and fear and move towards a state of happiness and freedom. By understanding the nature of our experience and through the awareness of things as they are, we free ourselves from anger, envy, hatred and greed, not because they are forbidden by the scriptures or by some god, or because they are 'sinful', but because they are unskilful states that drain our energy and make us unhappy.

The reality is that there are only actions and their consequences. All actions that have their roots in greed, hatred and delusion, that spring from self-centredness and from the search for permanence, that foster the harmful delusion of selfhood, are akusala karma, unskilful actions, and they produce dukkha. All those actions that are rooted in the virtues of generosity, love and wisdom are kusala karma, skilful or meritorious actions, and they are conducive to health, happiness and wisdom.

But these suggestions have to be considered only as pointers, and need to be worked out with honesty by us. The Buddhist traditions may have come out with amended yet strict ethical principles—some of which may even sound like commandments—but they are far from adequate for our times. In two thousand years, the world has changed much and radically. Our lives are much more complex and complicated compared with life during the Buddha's time. Although human emotions remain the same, 'negative' emotions have gathered a great deal of momentum over time, and now manifest in complex ways.

So, if the Buddha is to return today, he is unlikely to find us unusual or very different from the people of his times. And again, he would perhaps offer the same advice he gave to the Kalamas. A Buddha or a sage cannot give a set of ethical codes for people to practise for all time. He cannot provide a blueprint for good living and happiness. He can only point out errors in our thinking and practices and offer some vital clues as to how we could explore and find what is right for us.

We live in a harsh and complicated world and it is but a reflection of what we are. Being what we are, split from inside, we have created structures of belief and faith that have become the source of conflict, violence and sorrow. All our revolutions and ideas of creating a new society haven't touched the core of our divisive self. The great leaders of humanity have come and gone and their moral exhortations have not helped either.

Yet, whilst the social and environmental consequences of our way of living make the search for alternatives, for different peaceful, non-violent and non-exploitative ways of being and doing things more urgent, that search seems to lack conviction and strength. It seems that, fundamentally, the mind, founded on conflict and a divisive consciousness, which is self-protective and bourgeois by its very nature, is not the instrument to bring about a new society. Conflict, violence and sorrow shall be the curse and burden of our living unless the mind that has woven this web of conflict goes quiet and still.

The core of the Buddha's teaching is directed towards this awareness about the machinations of the mind and its problems.

The eightfold path or the twenty-four higher precepts given in the *Brahmajala Sutta* would be of little meaning and value when considered in isolation from his teaching on the nature of the human mind and experience. The ethical path is not merely directed towards strengthening 'the feeble altruism of human nature' but, more importantly, to loosen the grip of the binary mind so that the individual opens up to the possibility of freeing himself from fear and greed, from the dualistic mode of living in the world.

In short, moral exhortation in itself cannot take us far, cannot solve the problem of living. However much we may shout from rooftops about the need for new and more emancipatory politics, for better and more equitable models of development, for love and compassion in our lives, however much we may amend or even create new social and political structures, the intended goal will remain a dream, at best an ideal, unless the bourgeois mind undergoes a transformation, unless we attain prajna, wisdom, the awareness of the non-dual reality.

The practice of the eightfold path is for the sake of attaining bodhi or prajna. 'The other paramitas [perfections or excellences]', argues T.R.V. Murti, 'cannot even be paramitas without prajna-paramita ... It is prajna-paramita that can complete them, make each of them a paramita—a perfection.'[6] Without prajna, the practice of virtues, of any and every dhamma, is fated to be on shaky ground, beset by doubts and conflicts, but with prajna, virtues come naturally, without effort. Hence, with regard to the attempt of reducing the dhamma to a moral code, the Buddha warns:

> It is in respect only of trifling things, of matters of little value, of mere morality, that an ignorant man, when praising the Tathagata, would speak.

Bhikkhus, besides morality there are other dhammas, which are profound, hard to see, hard to comprehend, tranquil, noble ... The Tathagata has set them forth after realization of these dhammas by himself ... Anyone wishing to praise correctly the true virtues of the Tathagata should do so in terms of these dhammas ...[7]

THE WAY OUT

The mind is the problem. All our noble ideas and profound ideals have not percolated to the cellular structure of our being but have remained in the field of (idealistic) thinking. Under our skin, we have remained barbaric. That is the animal trait in us and we haven't been able to escape it despite our cultural, political and technological progress. The core of our being remains dualistic and animalistic.

If this is the truth, no matter what we do for years and for generations to come, there is not going to be a fundamental change in us because it is not a question of trying to find new concepts, new beliefs and new values, however radical or profound they may appear to be. We may go on changing human institutions infinitely and yet, as Aurobindo warned, the 'imperfections' will break through all our institutions. There must be another way.

'If you end this structure [the thought-structure, the 'I'], this continuity inside of you, once and for all,' says U.G. Krishnamurti, 'then there is a possibility because you are affecting the whole of the human consciousness. You may not see the result immediately. This explosion is bound to affect the whole humanity. These explosions are taking place every moment, it goes on and on. This seems to be the only way to change, to transform the world, that is, if at all you can help. This is real compassion that helps. The other way is not possible.'[8]

This is the crux of the Buddha's teaching as well. This is the 'dhamma', profound, tranquil, noble and hard to understand. This is the way: to loosen the grip of the mind, to break its continuity and let the creative energies locked up inside us express themselves and take us out of this cul-de-sac.

> Form is not yours, give it up. Sensation, perception, the formation and consciousness are not yours. Give them up ... When one is freed of all this, passion fades out. With the fading of passion, one is liberated. When liberated, there is awareness that one is liberated. Birth is exhausted, the holy life has been lived out, what can be done is done, of this there is no more beyond.[9]

A Buddha, a Christ, an Anandamayi Ma, a Ramana Maharshi or a U.G. Krishnamurti *is* the new society, the new world, the change for which humanity has been yearning and struggling for thousands of years through its religions and ethical principles, however flawed and erroneous these may have been. This world is possible, for every human being is a potential sage, a potential Buddha. But the potential cannot be realized by imitating the lives of the sages, creating structures of belief around their teaching and forcing this on people. Beliefs—the mind essentially, which is bourgeois and self-protective by its nature, is what separates us from others and from everything that is there.

Every human being is unique and unparalleled, but we ignore that fact and try to put everybody in a common mould, creating what we call the greatest common factor. Our education, religion, culture and politics are geared towards producing copies of socially acceptable models and, in the process, destroying that unique, living quality in a child, in every human being, that is yearning to blossom and express itself.

'The human animal has to flower into a human being,' says U.G. Krishnamurti.

And this can happen only when the animal content of the brain is quiet or becomes quiet through the process of evolution. But the process of evolution is retarded or delayed because of the culture, because of our anxiety to shape man according to a pattern, a model, or an idea or belief. So something has to be done, but then we continue to live the life of ideas of the mind and hence it is very difficult to grasp this.[10]

Dukkha
The Birth of the Self

In Buddhism as well as in the Upanishads and Advaita Vedanta, avidya is seen as the root cause of sorrow, but there is a difference where Buddhism is concerned. According to the Upanishads and Advaita Vedanta, the cause of duality and suffering is the ignorance of the unity of atman and Brahman. In Buddhism, it is the conditioned knowledge and the search for permanence that is the cause of attachment and suffering.

Further, the Upanishads/Advaita Vedanta and Buddhism assert that Truth or the Absolute is indescribable and inexpressible, and no category of thought applies to it. They both concur that it is avidya that invests Truth with namaroopa, name and form, and conceptualizes what cannot be expressed, what is paramartha satya, beyond phenomena. However, in Advaita Vedanta, although Brahman is inexpressible, there is a stubborn insistence that 'it' is knowable, realizable, for 'it' is svayamprakasha, self-evident and svasamvedya, self-revealed.

On the contrary, in Buddhism, according to Madhyamika

philosophy in particular, Truth is neither one nor many, neither permanent nor momentary, neither subject nor object; rather, it is indeterminate and unknowable. Any attempt to conceptualize Truth as 'this' or 'not this' is a case of vikalpa, imagination, or conceptual construction.

And so it is argued that this very faculty of knowing, of the intellect, which is rooted in duality, needs to be purified by giving up all views. But this 'no views about reality' should not be taken as 'a no-reality view'; it is just that nirvana or the Tathagata cannot and should not be theorized about.[1] This would be a futile exercise or viparyasa, a cognitive distortion.

PRATITYA-SAMUTPADA

Pratitya-samutpada (Paticca-samuppada in Pali), variously rendered into English as 'conditioned co-production', 'dependent origination', 'conditioned arising', 'conditioned genesis' and 'interdependent arising', is central to Buddhist doctrine, especially to the discourse on anatma, doctrine of no-self, and nirvana. Basically, pratitya-samutpada means that phenomena arise together in a mutually interdependent web of cause and effect. In other words, all phenomena are conditioned and arise and cease in a determinate series. This is actually common to all schools of Buddhism.

> From Ignorance as condition spring Mental Formation
> [samskaras],
> From Mental Formations springs Consciousness,
> From Consciousness spring Name and Form,
> From Name and Form spring Sense Gates
> From Sense Gates springs Contact,
> From Contact springs Sensation,

> From Sensation springs Craving,
> From Craving springs Attachment,
> From Attachment springs Becoming,
> From Becoming springs Birth,
> From Birth spring old age and death, grief, lamentation,
> suffering, dejection and despair.[2]

'This is how life arise, exists and continues,' declare Buddhist scholars and monks.[3] Before we continue, it needs to be pointed out here that the use of the word 'life', even words such as 'phenomena', 'world' and 'existence' are problematic. We have to distinguish between *life* and *living*. The above words are all ideations, abstractions of our experience of the world; we do not know the world as it truly is. We only know it through our personal experience of it. And we cannot 'know' about life in its totality, for it is a movement, forever in flux. It can never be captured by the mind, let alone having its origin understood by us.

So we need to see pratitya-samutpada as an attempt to theorize not the nature of the world or the nature of existence but the nature of the mind. In fact, it focuses on the birth of the mind and thereby samsara. It is not and cannot be a theory of causation. For, if we take the twelve links mentioned above literally, we fall under the illusion that things happen one after the other. It is not that way, since it is not possible to say this comes first and that next. It is actually a simultaneous process. 'When this exists, that comes to be; with the arising of this, that arises. When this does not exist, that does not come to be; with the cessation of this, that ceases.'[4]

The birth of the self or self-consciousness is the beginning of duality, formations, name and form, the 'I' and the 'other'. With the arising of the self, samsara arises, duality arises.

And hence there are desire and fear, joy and suffering, birth and death. This is the Wheel of Life (bhavacakka in Pali, bhavachakra in Sanskrit), involving the play of emotions, the cycle of birth and death. In actuality, it means the birth and continuity of the mind.

Let me reiterate that pratitya-samutpada as a logical-causal chain, illustrating in a linear fashion the preconditions of suffering that can be analysed and eliminated according to a strictly codified pattern of meditation and behaviour, is misleading. Many books on the teaching of the Buddha indulge in such an unproductive and wearisome exercise, creating the illusion that this is the way things have come into existence.

And, to bolster up this position, it is said that Siddhartha Gautama became enlightened under the bodhi tree when he fully realized the profound truth of pratitya-samutpada. As I have already explained, this is true but only in the sense that the 'realization' was an act of *seeing* and not the result of—as presented in most narratives—an epistemological penetration, because the mind cannot penetrate there; rather, the realization is the result of the cessation of the intellect, the movement of the self, which is the 'causal chain'.

The 'I' is the coordinator, the one who links thoughts and creates the illusion of continuity when, in actuality, there is no continuity. It is through this linking that mental formations, the craving and clinging, the entire business of dukkha, arises.

Pratitya-samutpada and the different forms of reflection and meditation such as bhakti yoga, jnana yoga, Satori (Zen) and Tao are all optimistic methods, deployed to break that chain or 'bondage' if you like. For that matter, most religious or spiritual disciplines are (supposedly) geared towards weakening and (hopefully) breaking that link. These techniques may work in loosening the grip of the mind, but ultimately what actually breaks the continuity remains unknown. From the reports of the experiences of sages, what we know is that once this link is broken, that is, the division in consciousness or the self disappears, the human finds himself in a state where there is no dukkha, because the continuity, which is what samsara is all about, is gone.

This understanding, which involves *seeing*, is not just difficult but impossible to transmit. So the sages, it seems, can only offer upayas, tricks or techniques that may trigger the process of change, but there is no guarantee. These tools and techniques are only signposts, a finger pointing to the moon.

J. KRISHNAMURTI ON CONDITIONING

Many Buddhist monks and scholars believe that J. Krishnamurti's teaching was all about pratitya-samutpada, that is, about conditioning and freedom from conditioning. In a sense, that may well be the case, but what is more important to see is the way he cut short the approach and pared it down to its bare facts. His observation that there is conditioning and there is freedom from conditioning is as to the point as the Buddha's exhortation: there is dukkha and there is the cessation of dukkha.

Human beings are conditioned. The whole web of their behavioural pattern, outlook, activities, contradictory states of mind, emotions, the inventions of gods and beliefs, the constant battle in the whole field of human consciousness is simply the outcome of this conditioned mind. And this conditioned mind has evolved through millennia—through wars, tears, sorrow, depression and elation—all that makes up our consciousness. 'Without the content, consciousness, as we know it, does not exist.'[5]

The content of consciousness is consciousness; it is always conditioned. Nevertheless, J. Krishnamurti avers that there is a state of consciousness or tranquillity that is not conditioned, where there is no centre such as 'I'. This is what the Buddha calls the 'unborn, unarisen'. It is the self that prevents one from being in that state of tranquillity or what may be called pure consciousness. But '... as long as the mind is holding on to a structure, a method, a system, there is no freedom. As long as the mind is caught in that, it can never be free.'[6]

So, J. Krishnamurti suggests that with the understanding of its conditioning, with the choiceless awareness of its own responses as thought and feeling, tranquillity comes to the mind. What this means is that it is only if we are aware of inward insufficiency and live with it without escape, accepting it wholly, that we will discover an extraordinary tranquillity, a tranquillity which is not put together or made up by thought.

U.G. KRISHNAMURTI: SEEING IS ENDING

U.G. Krishnamurti turns the whole discourse upside down so that we drop our cumbersome baggage and look at the issue straight in the eye.

We cannot know the origin of thought, much less the origin of life, he asserts. What we know is that there is thought, there is desire and there is the problem of living. Thought takes its birth when there is a demand, a want; that is the wheel of becoming, becoming something other than what we are, escaping from what is there. *This* is the whole problem, the conflict we are caught in; this is the cause of our sorrow.

We also know that all the techniques offered to us to lead us to liberation are just various *paths*. And we jump from one path to another, one technique to another. But if we are ruthlessly honest with ourselves, we will know that all this helps us up to a point and then we are back to the starting point. For years we struggle through these sadhanas and yet there is no fundamental change, for the core of our being remains unchanged.

So self-inquiry or our attempt to get rid of our conditioning is not the way. It is futile and absurd, warns U.G. Krishnamurti. We cannot know the content of consciousness because it simply is too vast and deep, with millions of years of momentum behind it. It is like taking a cup to empty the ocean.

We *stop* there, with the awareness that the one who is looking at conditioned thought is also conditioned. Any movement away from this fact is only further conditioning. 'You can't do a thing,' says U.G. Krishnamurti, and it sounds hopeless and terrible, but once we understand this supreme fact we are relieved of the burden and tyranny of knowledge, of knowing that which cannot be known.

Therefore, there is no such thing as an unconditioned mind; the mind is already always conditioned. Conditioning is tradition. Tradition is the self. No matter how we may modify or tweak or shape it, it continues. 'Every thought that is born has to die,' U.G. Krishnamurti points out.

> If a thought does not die, it cannot be reborn. It has to die, and with it you die. But you don't die with each thought and breath. You hook up each thought with the next, creating a false continuity. It is that continuity that is the problem ... So, unconditioning yourself has no meaning, no validity. What you have to be free from is the very desire to be free from conditioning.

Once we see this fact with the whole of our being, things fall into their natural rhythm: 'There is nothing to do, there is nothing to control, there is nothing to ask. You don't have to do a thing. *You* are finished.'[7]

Seeing is ending. To drive home this hard-to-understand, rather mind-blowing fact is the burden of the Buddha's teaching as well. Here is what he says to Ananda:

> Even if you succeed in putting an end to all seeing, hearing, feeling and knowing, and so preserve inner quiet, the shadow of [your] differentiation of things [dharma/samsaric phenomena] still remains.
>
> I do not want you to hold that this is not mind, but you should examine it carefully and minutely: that which continues to possess discerning nature even in the absence of sense data is really your mind; on the other hand if this discerning nature ceases with sense data, this is merely the shadow of [your] differentiation of them, for they are not permanent and when they cease to exist, so does this [so-called] mind, like the hair of a tortoise and the horns of a hare. If your mind can so easily cease to be, who will then realize the patient endurance of the unborn, unconditioned? [8]

The mind will not cease so easily, it cannot. It is not in the nature of the mind to be quiet, to fall dead. Even during meditation it is not quiet for, as the Buddha points out, 'the shadow of (your) differentiation of things (dharma/samsaric phenomena) still remains.' Extending the idea, as it were, U.G. Krishnamurti would say that the mind pervades the body. It is embedded in every cell. So, merely quieting the brain is not the answer. The whole organism has to become silent, and that is possible only when every cell in the body is cleansed of the mind, which has superimposed itself on the body. Only then the birth and continuity of the self, of dukkha, the bhavachakra, ceases to be.

Self-inquiry and yoga may all be necessary and valid but up to a point; after that, all these techniques become counterproductive and have to be dropped. In other words, pratitya-samutpada or any of these techniques as a method of inquiry and sadhana can loosen the grip of the 'chain', the self, but cannot break the chain or stop the wheel of becoming. The very search must end, the mind must go quiet; as U.G. Krishnamurti would put it, '*You* must stop for the sorrow to end.'

Where Is the Mind Located?

V.S. Ramachandran, brain researcher and the author of the widely acclaimed book *Phantoms in the Brain*, believes that the mind is located in the brain. He is of the view that questions such as 'What is the Self?', 'Do we have free will?', and 'What is consciousness?' can now be approached and explained empirically. He is certain that all our emotions and thoughts, ambitions and religious sentiments, and our very sense of self are all the activity of little specks of jelly in the brain. Therefore, it is only in the brain that we can eventually hope to find the answers.[1]

This is a tall claim largely based on experiments done on willing volunteers and patients with strange behavioural patterns. However, this is understandable as this is how science proceeds and develops, and it has enriched our understanding of life and the world. However, to jump to the conclusion that the self is located in the brain is unwarranted. Over the centuries, the sages who have a deeper understanding of the nature of the mind have consistently and categorically stated that the brain is not the seat of the self and it is not the generator of the thought process; it is the storehouse of memory and not its manufacturer. But we'll come to that in a while.

Even in more recent books, Ramachandran exhibits a stubborn hope to discover the location of the self in the brain, although he admits—which unwittingly takes him a little closer to the 'insights' of the sages—that from what he has learnt so far, 'the self consists of many components, and the notion of one unitary self may well be an illusion'.[2]

New Age theorists, however, are suspicious of this kind of overenthusiasm of neuroscientists like Ramachandran, and reject their findings on the ground that you cannot really reduce human experiences or human consciousness to purely neural mechanisms. This alternative theory also suggests that these scientists succeed only in explaining away the complex relationship between the nature of the human brain and consciousness.

The mind is not just an activity of the brain; the whole organism is involved in the process of the functioning of the mind. Representing such a view held by many alternative theorists and scientists, Fritjof Capra suggests that the mind is not a thing but a process of cognition, which can be identified with the process of life itself. The brain is a specific structure through which this process operates. The relationship between mind and brain, therefore, is one between process and structure. 'The entire structure of the organism participates in the process of cognition, whether or not the organism has a brain and a higher nervous system.' For that matter, 'At all levels of life, beginning with the simplest cell, mind and matter, process and structure are inseparably connected.'[3]

THE NATURE OF THE MIND

The Buddha was residing at a large meeting hall in an ancient forest in Sravasti. With a great congregation of people in attendance, he explored with Ananda the location, nature and function of the mind, and if there is anything beyond.

> Buddha: 'Ananda, tell me, by what means did you behold me?'
>
> Ananda: 'I used my eyes and my mind.'
>
> Buddha: 'Then the true ground of beholding is to be sought in the mind and the eye. But what is the precise location of this mind and this sight?'
>
> Ananda: 'Everyone agrees that the mind is within the body and the eye is within the head.'
>
> Buddha: 'If the mind is within the body, then it would be acquainted with the inner parts of the body itself. But how is it then, that we never meet a man who is able to see his own internal organs? No, that the mind is located within the body cannot be maintained.'[4]

Then Ananda asserts, though feebly, that the mind is located outside the body. When that position is also taken apart by the Buddha, Ananda wonders if the mind could be located somewhere between the two or even embedded in the senses! The Buddha negates those views, saying they are only assumptions without any basis in reality. Not knowing what position to take, in sheer frustration, Ananda asks:

> I have heard the assertion that the nature of the mind is such that it could not be said to be within the body, nor without it, nor in the middle point, but that the mind in its very nature is without a local habitation. I would be glad to know whether I may define the mind as that which is 'indefinite' and 'without partiality'.[5]

After the Buddha systematically deconstructs all of Ananda's positions with regard to the location of the mind, what gets more or less established at this stage of the dialogue is that the mind *cannot* be located. We cannot say it exists in the brain or anywhere else in the body, nor can we prove that it exists outside.

Interestingly, in our times, U.G. Krishnamurti's position with regard to the location and nature of the mind was not very different from that of the Buddha's. In fact, his discovery reconfirms what the Buddha said of the mind 2,600 years ago. Challenging the neuroscientists' view that the mind is located in the brain, U.G. Krishnamurti asserted that thoughts are not really spontaneous or self-generated; actually, thoughts always come from outside the organism, in the sense that they originate due to external influence. In other words, the brain is not really a creator of thought; it is just a container and a reactor. What the brain does is to translate sensory perceptions within the framework of memory, while its natural function is to take care of the needs of the physical organism and maintain its sensitivity.

Further, he asserted that despite all the experiments that brain physiologists and psychologists are doing to locate the seat of human consciousness, they will never be able to find out. Nor will it be possible for anybody to discover all of consciousness—it is too vast. The genetic aspect is only part of it.

Now, returning to the dialogue, the Buddha then proceeds to discuss the nature of this mind and why it does not belong to Ananda. He also shows how it is an error to think so.

Buddha stretched out his hand and drew his fingers into a fist. Then he asked Ananda 'What do you see?'

Ananda: 'I see the Tathagata raising his arm and bending his fingers into a fist.'

Buddha: 'Now, what is the instrument by which you see all this?'

Ananda: 'I and all present see this by the use of our eyes.'

Buddha: 'If it is your eyes which see the fist, of what account is the mind?'

Ananda: 'I take it that the mind is the power by which I investigate.'

Buddha: 'No, no, Ananda, this is not your mind.'

Ananda: 'If this is not my mind, tell me what it may be called.'

Buddha: 'This is but the perception of vain and false qualities which, under the guise of your true nature, has from the first deceived you.' And then he adds, 'Tathagatha ever says, every phenomenon that presents itself to our knowledge is but a manifestation of the mind ... which is the true substratum of all ... Thus, while you now hear me declaring the law, it is because of the sounds you hear that there is a discriminating process within you; yet, after all sounds have disappeared, there still continues a process of thought within, in which memory acts as principal element, so that there is a mind acting as it were on the mere shadows of things.'[6]

The last few lines are very significant. What the Buddha is saying is that even when there is no sound, no talking and listening, the thought process continues. As U.G. Krishnamurti would say, the vocal chords are functioning although we may not sense it. Even when thinking has apparently come to an end, for instance, while meditating or when we are in deep sleep, we cannot say the mind is absent or thought has disappeared.

And then the Buddha hammers in the fact that the mind Ananda has been so proudly referring to actually does not belong to him. He says that the perception that 'this is my mind ... this is me' is false, and has 'from the first, deceived you.' In effect, the Buddha is saying that there are only thoughts but the identification with these thoughts creates the illusion of 'I'. This 'I' acts, as it were, on mere 'shadows', by which is meant the past, memory, dependent on external phenomena. To drive home the point, later in the passage (not quoted here), the Buddha gives the instance of a person suffering from a cataract in the eye. As a result, his perception of the world is distorted. Similarly, our perception of the world is conditioned by defective vision and it is so because of the 'disease' called ignorance.

THE WORLD MIND

To explicate this matter in clearer terms, U.G. Krishnamurti uses the term 'world mind' or 'thought sphere' to explain the nature of this 'I' or the 'self' (advocates of memetic theory may kindly note). The world mind constitutes the totality of thoughts, feelings and experiences of humankind.

> The world mind is that which has created you and me. This world mind is self-perpetuating and its only interest is to maintain its continuity, which it can do only through the creation of what we call individual minds—your mind and my mind, though there is no such thing as your mind and my mind ... Without the help of that knowledge, you have no way of experiencing yourself as an entity. We are caught up in this vicious circle, namely, of knowledge giving you the experience, and the experience in turn strengthening and fortifying that knowledge which has been put into us during the course of our life.[7]

Knowledge is all that is there. The self is nothing but the totality of this vast, inherited knowledge that is passed on from generation to generation through genes as well as culture. This is how human living has gone on over millions of years, but we have no way at all of finding out the seat of thought or human consciousness. Within this consciousness also survive 'plant consciousness' and 'animal consciousness'.[8]

What we think as *my* consciousness is not different from social consciousness. The world is not different from us; we *are* the world. Every thought we think, every feeling we feel is related to society, it is part of society. The self that we think is unique and unparalleled is but an illusion, in the sense it is an artificially created structure from the world mind, the beginningless thought structure.

So, all that can be said in summary is that the birth of the self marked the division in the primordial unitary consciousness, and from then on 'every phenomenon that presents itself to our knowledge is but a manifestation of the mind.'[9] The world is manifested and perceived as real under the influence of *habit-energy* (memory and vasanas, mental dispositions) that have been accumulated since the *beginning*. Notions such as causation, primary elements, Personal Soul, Supreme Spirit, God and Creator are all creations of the imagination, manifestations of the mind. It is like a wheel of fire made by a revolving firebrand: there is no wheel truly, but one imagines there is because one is ignorant.

No-Mind or Pure Consciousness

The *Mandukya Upanishad* is the shortest of the major Upanishads, with just twelve verses, but it is the one on which Gaudapada, considered the paramaguru in the Advaita Vedanta tradition and a crypto-Buddhist by many religious scholars, wrote his commentary. The *Mandukya Upanishad* is a premier text where we find perhaps the earliest attempt to formulate a 'psychology' or science of the mind. And this text, at least those parts of it that deal with turiya, fourth state, could not have been the result of logical or discursive thinking but a piercing insight and an abstraction of the nature of 'no-mind'.

The mystic syllable *aum* is linked to three states of consciousness: jagrata, the state of waking consciousness, where we experience externally through our mind and sense organs; svapna, the state of dreaming where inward experiences are available; and sushupti, dreamless sleep, where consciousness seems to gather in upon itself and lie quiet.

However, in all three states the self or ego remains very much active and is the basis of all the experiences.

In the first two states, waking and dreaming are conditioned by the dual nature of the self. In the state of dreamless sleep, one is not conscious of external or internal objects, but that does not mean consciousness or the self is absent. Divided consciousness or the self is the constant factor in all the three states.

TURIYA

Turiya or 'turiya avastha' is the fourth state, the substratum of the other three states. The *Mandukya Upanishad* says that this state is 'unseen and ineffable, ungraspable, featureless, unthinkable and unnamable'. Turiya is also referred to as 'atyanta sunyata', absolute emptiness.

> The fourth, turiya, say the wise, is not subjective experience, nor objective experience, nor experience intermediate between these two, nor is it a negative condition which is neither consciousness nor unconsciousness. It is not the knowledge of the senses, nor is it relative knowledge, nor yet inferential knowledge. Beyond the senses, beyond the understanding, beyond all expression, is The Fourth. It is pure unitary consciousness, wherein awareness of the world and of multiplicity is completely obliterated. It is ineffable peace.[1]

Western psychology, from the time of Freud, Adler and Jung to the present day, has no notion of No-Mind or Pure Consciousness. Categories such as the conscious, subconscious and unconscious may be useful for understanding and explaining the functioning of the mind at different levels. They are also used to talking about dreams, behavioural patterns and transpersonal experiences, but they don't help us to understand the state of being which is not of the mind, where there is no dreaming and thinking, a state without images and self-reflection, and without the operation of will and experience as we understand in the framework of Western psychology.

The study of different kinds of religious experiences and higher states of consciousness by Western religious scholars did take them closer to the edge of the mind, but that did not throw any light on the state of being where the mind is not involved. Their use of terms such as 'trance', 'rapture', 'ecstasy' and 'oceanic feeling' gave a sense of the higher states of consciousness but that could hardly give us an idea of the state of being the sages describe. The turiya avastha is not a higher state of consciousness or a mystical experience; in fact, it is not a state of experience at all. It is the end of the experiencing entity. It is not a state beyond the mind but a state that is not *of the mind*. Here, the self is absent and there is just pure awareness.

Commenting on turiya avastha in his *Karika,* Gaudapada says:

> All the multiple objects, comprising the movable and the immovable, are perceived by the mind alone. For duality is never perceived when the mind ceases to act.
>
> When the mind, after realizing the knowledge that Atman alone is real, becomes free from imaginations and therefore does not cognize anything, for want of objects to be cognized, it ceases to be the mind.[2]

Employing classical Hindu terminology, Ramana Maharshi says:

> Atman is the light of *Sat, Chit, Ananda. Visva, Taijasa* and *Prajna* are the denominations of the experiencer in the waking, dream and deep sleep states respectively. The same individual

underlies all of them. They do not therefore represent the True Self, which is pure *Sat, Chit, Ananda*.[3]

And yet, Ramana Maharshi would assert that the atman is the basis of all the experiences in that it remains the witness and the support of them all, although the Supreme Reality is different from the three states of waking, dreaming and deep sleep. Sometimes, Ramana Maharshi also used other Hindu terms such as 'nirvikalpa samadhi', 'sahaja samadhi' and 'turiyatita' to describe that state of pure consciousness.

PURE CONSCIOUSNESS

Buddhism discusses the different states of consciousness in terms of four jhanas, the fourth being a state of consciousness untouched by thought. Some schools of Buddhism have made a further division of these four states into rupa jhana, material state and arupa jhana, immaterial or formless dimensions, and speak of the *ninth* jhana as the ultimate state of being. But it is enough for us to understand that there is a state of being where the mind is not involved, where the binary opposites and all frontiers have disappeared. Describing the fourth jhana, the Buddha says:

> With the abandoning of pleasure and stress, he enters and remains in the fourth jhana: purity of equanimity and mindfulness, neither-pleasure-nor-pain. He sits, permeating the body with a pure, bright awareness, so that there is nothing of his entire body unpervaded by pure, bright awareness.[4]

'... there is nothing of his entire body unpervaded by pure, bright awareness' should give us some clue about the fourth state. It is not a state of experience or even a state of being, since all forms have dissolved in 'bright awareness'. There is no body, no mind and no world—only bright awareness!

Tathata, 'suchness' or 'thusness'; satyata, the state of being true; bhutata, the state of being real; dharmadhatu, realm of truth; nirvana; advaya; nirodha, cessation; animitta, formless; sunyata, emptiness are the various expressions used to give us some idea of this fourth state of being.

Avoiding both Hindu and Buddhist terminologies, U.G. Krishnamurti uses simple words to indicate the inexpressible, highlighting the fact that it is not a mental state but a physical and physiological state of being. But in all enlightenment traditions hitherto, whether Hindu or Buddhist, the fourth state always has been explained or understood in psychological terms, though it is not of the mind. That must change in the face of incontrovertible evidence offered by U.G. Krishnamurti. His emphasis that the natural state is a physical and physiological state of being must open up a radically new understanding of turiya avastha or dharmadhatu. U.G. Krishnamurti says:

This awareness is a burning thing. The observer, the observed, the experiencer, the experienced, the experiencing— everything is burnt and they are the same thing …

Why are you separating them, they are all one and the same thing. Swapna, Jagrata and Sushupti—they are same, not three different states of being. They are the three aspects of the same thing; when you breakthrough them it is what you call the turiya state.

I am alert and awake. In that state what is there is pure consciousness, awareness, where there are no choices of any kind; just awareness. It is like a camera lens being exposed, it is just taking pictures, there is nobody there interpreting these pictures; there is no good and bad, beautiful and ugly, no choice involved.

There are thousands of sensations bombarding your body … Thoughts are there all the time. This [body] is an electromagnetic field. Thoughts are vibrations and you are decoding them all the time. Here [in the natural state] there is no decoding, no translation of these vibrations and the whole of your being is filled with that vibration.

It is the same with the listening mechanism. There is no music for me; only sound, vibrations, whether it is Beethoven's symphony or the barking of a dog.

There is no sleep for me, because there is no division in this consciousness as wakefulness and sleep, in the sense that there is nobody inside to say now I am awake, now I am sleeping, breathing ... There is only perception, pure perception without the perceiver. That is the end and the beginning of life.

This is not a mental state. This is pure and simple physical and physiological state of being. There is awareness, pure consciousness; it is all one, for there are no frontiers here, it is the undivided state of consciousness, the unitary movement of life.[5]

That is Aware of Itself

You may ask if there is really such a state of being where the mind as we know is totally absent. Is it possible for someone to function in the world with absolutely no conflict or fear, without naming and forming images? How are we to understand this?

We will not be able to understand this state of being within a strictly Western psychological framework, where the mind can be understood and explained only in terms of the tripartite structure of the id, ego and superego. Though there are today psychologists who may have widened the tripartite structure or even moved away from it to explain transpersonal and mystical experiences, they are yet to reckon with the state of being or awareness where there is no thinking-feeling subject and therefore no object, no cognitive process in operation.

The sages may be the living examples of that state of being, of pure awareness but still, the question may be asked: How does a Buddha or a U.G. Krishnamurti know that he is in a state of 'bright awareness' or 'pure consciousness'? If the fourth state is really indescribable, how then can it be described using labels? Who is describing it? Isn't it the mind?

Masters like U.G. Krishnamurti clarify that in the state of undivided consciousness there is no mind, no 'I' in operation at all and therefore there is no question of describing that state. Also, words cannot describe that undifferentiated state of being, for words by their very nature divide things up and frame reality; it would be like trying to catch the void with your hand. Nevertheless, a master does bring the *factual* mind into play in order to abstract that state in words, so we get a sense of what it is or is not. Indeed, this talking is a disturbance, like ripples in an otherwise placid lake. Still, he speaks in order to communicate what is actually incommunicable. When a challenge or question is thrown at such a being, the factual mind—factual memory as opposed to emotional memory—comes into operation. Once the required task has been performed, it burns itself out without leaving a trace behind, and the master reverts to the state of pure awareness, of silence. It is a paradox.

The Upanishads resolve this paradox by simply stating, 'That is aware of Itself.' This means that the Self is beheld by itself alone. The Buddha says, '… the perfection of wisdom is not something that thought has access to,' and yet uses terms such as 'unborn', 'unarisen', 'unconditioned' or 'emptiness' to give us a sense of what it is. U.G. Krishnamurti merely says, 'Not that there is somebody who is aware of life, but life is aware of its own incredible depths.'

It is like being a silent witness. It is not unconsciousness; it is not external consciousness nor internal consciousness; yet, it is not the absence of consciousness either. This is consciousness without a centre and without frontiers. It is Pure Consciousness. Nothing more can be said about it. The *Mundaka Upanishad*, however, describes this mystery with the metaphor of two birds. Two birds of golden plumage, inseparable companions, are perched on a tree. They are the individual self and the Immortal Self. 'The former tastes of the sweet and bitter fruits of the tree, the latter, tasting of neither, calmly observes.'[6]

Is There a Soul?

In the Upanishads and the Advaita Vedanta texts, the 'self' is generally used for the ego, the mind, the thinking-feeling subject, while the 'Self' refers to what is beyond the ego or the mind; it is the higher self, the atman, which is said to be essentially same as Brahman: the source and ground of all existence.

Buddhism deals only with the 'self' and does not talk about the higher self. The Buddhist's position is that it is pointless to discuss whether the soul (although the term 'soul' may have different connotations, it is used here to mean the higher self) exists or not, because even if it exists, it cannot be known; it is avyakta, inexpressible. For, in the state of being where the mind is absent, who can tell what it is and what it is not? Therefore, all assertions or affirmations about the soul are seen as projections of an insecure mind, which is still part of becoming and hence subject to suffering and rebirth.

According to Buddhism, only the material processes (of the body) and the mental processes that make up the mind exist, but then they do not belong to us, for they arise in dependence on conditions over which we have no control. In actuality, however, there is no centre, no self; it is an illusion. The self is only a label we attach to the aggregate of certain physical and psychical factors, but they have no independent existence. The self or the mind is put up by the five skandhas: rupa, vijnana, vedana, samjna and samskara; while rupa stands for the physical, the rest constitute the psychical elements of the self. What we call 'self-consciousness' or 'mental dispositions' are nothing but a combination of these factors or skandhas, and they are forever in a state of flux.

There are only a series of sensations, a play of the biochemical, so to say, which is put together by the mind into a form, a stream of ideas, and we imagine a common element or character underlying the stream and call it the Self or atman. This is only a trick of the insecure mind to anchor itself in something it believes to be permanent and immortal.

Philosophers might argue that the very idea of flux anticipates something that is not in a state of flux; therefore it is but right and philosophically valid to ask if there is something, say, an ultimate reality beyond. This is a classical Hindu position, deriving its authority from the Upanishadic affirmation that there is Brahman, which is beyond the phenomena. The Buddha did not speak about it, refusing to get into 'the shackles of theorizing'.[1] He simply took a position of silence.

NAGASENA'S THESIS

Nagasena was a Buddhist who lived in c. 150 BCE. His answers to questions posed by Milinda I, the Indo-Greek king of north-western India, are recorded in the *Milinda Panha*. In the dialogue, reproduced here, Nagasena shows how we construct the idea of the self, how it is an artificially erected entity and nothing more.

King Milinda asked Nagasena: 'How is your Reverence known, and what is your name, Sir?'

Nagasena: 'As Nagasena I am known, O great king, but this word "Nagasena" is just a denomination, a designation, a conceptual term, a mere name. For no real person can here be apprehended.'

Addressing the assembly, Milinda said, 'Now listen, you Greeks and monks, this Nagasena tells me that he is not a real person. How can I be expected to agree with that?'

And then turning to Nagasena, he continues, 'If no person can be apprehended in reality, who, then, I ask you, gives you what you require by way of robes, food, lodging, and medicines? What is it that consumes them? Who is it that guards morality, and practices meditation? For, if there were no person, there could be no merit or demerit; no doer of meritorious or demeritorious deeds, and no agent behind them; ... and no reward or punishment for them. If someone should kill you, O Venerable Nagasena, he would not commit any murder ...

'What then is this "Nagasena"? Is the hairs of the body, the nails, teeth, skin, muscles, sinews, bones, marrow, kidneys, heart, liver, serous membranes, spleen, lungs, intestines, stomach, excrement, the bile, phlegm, pus, blood, fat, tears, sweat, spittle, snot, fluid of the joints, urine or the brain in the skull? Are they this "Nagasena"?'

Nagasena: 'No, great king!'

Milinda: 'Or is form this "Nagasena", or feeling, perceptions, impulses or consciousness? Or is it the combination of form, feelings, perceptions, impulses and consciousness?'

Nagasena: 'No, great king!'

Milinda: 'Then is it outside the combination of form, feelings, perceptions, impulses and consciousness?'

Nagasena: 'No, great king!'

Milinda: 'Then, I can discover no Nagasena at all. Just a

mere sound is this "Nagasena", but who is the real Nagasena? Your Reverence has told a lie, has spoken a falsehood! There really is no Nagasena!'

Nagasena: 'Let me explain; but, first, tell me, how you arrived here. On foot or on a chariot?'

Milinda: 'I did not come on foot but on a chariot.'

Nagasena: 'If you have come on a chariot, then please explain to me what a chariot is. Is the pole, the wheels, the framework, the flagstaff, the yoke, the reins or the goadstick?'

Milinda: 'No, Sir!'

Nagasena: 'Then is it the combination of pole, axle, wheels, framework, flagstaff, yoke, reins and goad? Or is this "chariot" outside the combination of pole, axle, wheels, framework, flagstaff, yoke, reins and goad?'

Milinda: 'No, Sir!'

Nagasena: 'Then, I can discover no chariot at all. Just a mere sound is this "chariot". But what is the real chariot? You have not established its existence. Where is it? Your Majesty has told a lie, has spoken a falsehood! There really is no chariot!

Milinda: 'I have not, Nagasena, spoken a falsehood. For it is in dependence on the pole, the axle, the wheels, the framework, the flagstaff, etc., that there takes place this denomination "chariot", this designation, this conceptual term, a current appellation and a mere name.'

Nagasena: 'Your Majesty has spoken well about the chariot. It is just so with me. In dependence on the thirty-two parts of the body and the five skandhas there takes place this denomination "Nagasena", this designation, this conceptual term, a current appellation and a mere name. In ultimate reality, however, this person cannot be apprehended.'[2]

What Nagasena is doing here is to shift our attention from the needless and unproductive metaphysical discussion about whether there is an immortal soul to the human mind. There are only thoughts, no thinker; but we put these thoughts together in a frame and abstract from it an underlying immortal atman in the same way that we put together or assemble different parts into a shape and name it a chariot. In other words, there is only a series of sensations, put together by the mind into a form, a stream of ideas, and we imagine an immortal entity underlying the stream and call it the Self. This, to Nagasena, is an unproductive and illegitimate abstraction that creates a mere appearance, which we mistake for real.

THE UNKNOWN

Before we explore further, it is necessary that we examine the meaning and implication of the notion of soul/spirit. Etymologically speaking, it is said that atman in Sanskrit, psyche in Greek, anima and even spiritus in Latin mean 'breath'. If spirit or soul means 'breath' or 'breath of life', perhaps there isn't much to talk about it except to say, well, prana or 'breath' is the defining characteristic of all life forms.

But the notions of spirit or soul as found in the belief systems of the major religions and even mystical reports are quite complex and complicated and different from each other. The Hindu notion of atman is not the same as the Christian or Islamic Soul. But the one common defining characteristic of these different narratives of the soul is that it is regarded as an independent or separate entity; and in its relationship with God, mind and body, it is always privileged over the body.

The soul is pure and transcendental. The body is impure and mundane, subject to decay and death. It is something to be rejected, abandoned and transcended in order to come upon or realize and experience the soul. Despite all the hermeneutical attempts to overcome the dualism of body-soul, soul-god, one has to concede that this dualism between the body and soul is the bedrock on which all religions are built, and it continues to be the core of all their discourses.

The situation is pretty much the same with what goes under the name of spirituality. Isn't spirituality understood and expressed as something concerned not with the material or the mundane, but with the sacred, the divine? Isn't spirituality seen as an engagement with the soul as opposed to the body and external reality? This dichotomy between spirit and matter, body and soul, spirituality and materialism is the warp and woof of most religions and spiritual traditions.

In the light of this, it should now become clear as to why the Buddha—like the modern sages in our times—refused to talk about the existence, or otherwise, of the soul. Let me summarize:

- The notion of the soul is a view, a concept; like all concepts, it creates its opposites and thereby fragments reality. This dichotomy between body and mind, mind and spirit, spirituality and materiality and so on, can falsify the search at the very beginning and drive a seeker in the wrong direction:
- It is the trick of the (insecure, bourgeois) mind to seek a centre, an anchor in the so-called transcendent substance like the Purusha, God or Brahman;
- Even if there is God, it is unknown and unknowable. The divisive mind or thought cannot penetrate the unknown and so it gives up.

Hence the Buddha asks Ananda, 'If your mind can so easily cease to be, who will then realize the patient endurance of the Unborn?' Words such as 'unborn' and 'unarisen' are not concepts. It is only a manner of saying that the Buddhadhatu or nirvana cannot be described because there is no entity there to describe. One has to live through it. Yet, negative words or terms may be used to give us a sense of that state.

In the Upanishads, even though Atman-Brahman is described ad nauseam, the seers acknowledge that ultimately Brahman is beyond words, in the sense that it is not within the realm of knowledge and knowing. Therefore, the *Brihadaranyaka Upanishad* describes it negatively as 'neti, neti', 'not this, not this.'

If that is so, one may ask why this should be described at all in the first place if only to negate it? Why put a name on it? Why give it a form? If there is absolutely no reference point to *That* and therefore there is no way we can speak about it, shouldn't we just let go? As always, U.G. Krishnamurti's direct and lucid explanation of this mystery should clear whatever confusion we may still have. He says:

> That is the unknown and it will always remain the unknown. If it becomes part of your thought-structure, your knowledge, it has no meaning. You have destroyed the possibility of coming into that state. As long as this movement of thought is there, the other one is not there.
>
> The body is in a state of quiet, of relaxation, which you can call Bliss, Truth, Love, God or Reality or anything you like, but it is not that, because there is nobody looking at it. I look at that thing (microphone) there and I can bring out the word and say it is a microphone. But here, for this state of being, there is no word you can find to describe it. So the words Bliss, Love, God, Truth are all inadequate to express this state of being.[3]

Now let us hear what the Buddha says. Once, the Buddha dwelt at Rajagriha with a great gathering of monks. The Buddha spoke to Subhuti:

'Make it clear now, Subhuti, how the Bodhisattvas, the great beings go forth into perfect wisdom!'

Promptly, Sariputra said: 'Deep is the essential original nature of the dharmas [phenomena].'

The Buddha: 'Because it is unknown.'

Subhuti: 'Deep is the essential nature of perfect wisdom.'

The Buddha: 'Because its essential nature is pure and unknown, therefore has the perfection of wisdom a deep essential nature.'

Subhuti: 'Unknown is the essential nature of perfect wisdom.'

The Buddha: 'All dharmas are unknown in their essential nature and this essential nature of all dharmas is identical with the perfection of wisdom.'

Subhuti: 'Therefore all dharmas have the character of not having fully known by the Tathagata?'

The Buddha: 'All dharmas have one mark only, i.e., no mark. There are no two natures of dharma, but just one single one is the nature of all dharmas. And the nature of all dharmas is no-nature, and their no-nature is their nature. It is thus that all those points of attachment are abandoned.'

Subhuti: 'Deep, O Lord, is the perfection of wisdom and hard to understand.'

The Buddha: 'Because the perfection of wisdom is not something that thought ought to know, or that thought has access to.'[4]

Is There Rebirth?

What is rebirth? Is it the Self or soul being reborn or is it the ego that is taking birth again? Further, if the soul is eternal, pure and immutable, not affected or tainted by the doings of the ego, why would the soul need to be reborn? If the Atman-Brahman, as described in the *Katha Upanishad*, is 'unborn, eternal, permanent and ancient', it cannot be conceived of nor spoken about in terms of the cycles of birth and death. Extending this line of argument, Professor T. R. V. Murti writes:

> How does the acceptance of the atman—the unchanging permanent entity—explain karma, rebirth, memory and personal identity more plausibly? As the permanent soul is of one uniform immutable nature, it cannot have different volitions when different circumstances call for different actions ... A changing atman is a contradiction in terms.[1]

Or, if we accept a changing soul, there can be no valid argument for its 'immutable' nature.

Further, how çan an unchanging being like the soul remember anything at all? Memory is not merely continuity of consciousness but the knowing of an object as having been experienced in the past, and relating it to the present experience. So, how can atman, which is unchanging, immutable and without a beginning, have a past or even be related to it in any way?

Then there is another difficulty. If the psychological states like joy, pain and pleasure are transitory, how can these states belong to the unchanging soul? So, this whole theory of rebirth vis-à-vis the soul is hopelessly problematic. Perhaps the only way you can circumvent this problem—Hindu scholars and gurus indulge in it as a last resort—is to bring in the notion of maya and assert that it is all maya and ultimately unknowable.

Now, let's say it is not the Self but the ego that is reborn. If it is the ego or the self that is reborn, again the belief has no basis. But, no, not entirely, you might say. With regard to the belief in rebirth, both the Hindu and Buddhist enlightenment traditions ride on two horses, as it were. On the one hand, both these traditions assert that the self or the individuated ego is an illusion, that thoughts do not belong to the individual, therefore the individual per se does not exist; on the other hand, there is also the belief in both the traditions that the self survives death and hangs about in space or in a different realm, as it were, and after or within a certain period of time, it seeks a new body and is reborn. There are texts that go into details of how the self escapes the dead body and has its hibernation period on the astral plane before it gets hooked into a new body.

For instance, according to the *Satapatha Brahmana*, one who has the right knowledge and performs the prescribed religious and social duties or karmas scrupulously shall be fit for immortality, while the one who lacks knowledge and neglects his duties is subject to the endless cycles of births and deaths.

Karma means 'action' but, over the centuries, the law of

karma has come to mean the effects or consequences of our acts. 'Good' acts are rewarded with good birth and eventual immortality; 'bad' acts (not practising the moral codes, ignorance of the Vedas and Atman-Brahman, ignorance of the truth that nothing belongs to us and all phenomena are empty) are punished with the endless cycle of rebirth.

It seems there was no escape for Buddhism from incorporating this idea of rebirth into its philosophy, despite its doctrine of no-self. The laws of karma and rebirth were powerful ideas that seemed to justify the cause of suffering and the difference in the status and conditions of people. Thus, inevitably, early Buddhism worked its way into the heart of the people by popularizing the conception of rebirth by relating the previous births of the Buddha through the Jataka tales.

DID THE BUDDHA BELIEVE IN REBIRTH?

This belief in rebirth is inconsistent with the Buddha's denial of an enduring self. It damages and defeats the core teaching of the Buddha. Rhys Davids, the noted translator and scholar, observes,

> The position is so absolute ... Yet the position is also original, so fundamentally opposed to what is usually regarded as religious belief, both in India and elsewhere, that there is a great temptation to attempt to find a loophole through which at least a covert or esoteric belief in the soul, and in the future life can be recognized, in some sort of way, as part of so widely accepted a religious system. There is no loophole, and the efforts to find one have always met with unswerving opposition, both in the Pitakas themselves and in extra-canonical works.'[2]

We may wonder, therefore, how anybody could still justifiably credit the Buddha with a belief in transmigration. Yet, not very surprisingly, several Buddhist texts do reflect this contradiction. There have also been attempts by some scholars to dig into 'primitive' Buddhism to prove that the Buddha did believe in the existence of soul, and that 'anatmavada', soullessness was only a later addition. Against such a theory, scholars like T.R.V. Murti would argue that for every textual citation that apparently affirms the atman, there are ten or twenty which deny it with vehemence.[3]

Indeed, it remains a dilemma within the enlightenment traditions of both Buddhists and Hindus to this day. Within these traditions, there are scholars, gurus and monks to whom the doctrine of rebirth is neither a contradiction nor a dilemma to be resolved. S. Radhakrishnan, for example, reasons that because of karma, people are not alike, and without an explanation to justify things, 'people would feel themselves to be victims of an immense injustice'.[4] If even thinkers like S. Radhakrishnan must find it insuperably difficult to conceive of a moral philosophy devoid of all compensatory motives, it is easy to imagine the difficulty experienced in this matter by interpreters of an earlier epoch.[5]

What the Buddha says of the soul, the nature of the mind and experience are so transparently sound and simple that there should be no confusion about his position with regard to the idea of transmigration. Yes, he did speak of 'rebirth' but not in the sense of the soul or the self going through the cycle of birth and death until it is liberated. His point was radically different, and its implication should serve as a corrective to the popular understanding of 'rebirth' endorsed by gurus and scholars. This 'corrective' is available in various texts and needs to be explicated.

Once, Kutadanta, the head of the Brahmans in the village of Danamati, having approached the Blessed One respectfully, asked:

'You say, O Master, that beings are reborn; that they migrate in the evolution of life; and that subject to the law of karma we must reap what we sow. Yet you also teach the non-existence of the soul! Your disciples praise utter self-extinction as the highest bliss of nirvana. If I am merely a combination of the sankhara, my existence will cease when I die. If I am merely a compound of sensations and ideas and desires, whither can I go at the dissolution of the body?'

The Buddha said: 'O Brahman, you are religious and earnest. You are seriously concerned about your soul. Yet your work is in vain because you are lacking in the one thing that is needful. *There is rebirth of character, but no transmigration of a self* [italics mine]. Your thought-forms reappear, but there is no ego-entity transferred. The words uttered by a teacher are reborn in the scholar who repeats the words.

'Only through ignorance and delusion do men indulge in the dream that their souls are separate and self-existent entities. Your heart, O Brahman, is cleaving still to self; you are anxious about heaven but you seek the pleasures of self in heaven, and thus you cannot see the bliss of truth and the immortality of truth now.

'Listen, O Brahman, this body will be dissolved and no amount of sacrifice will save it. Therefore, you seek the life that is of the mind. Where self is, truth cannot be; yet when truth comes, self will disappear ... self is death and truth is life. The cleaving to self is a perpetual dying, while moving in the truth is partaking of nirvana, which is life everlasting.'[6]

There is no ambiguity in what the Buddha asserts: there is no soul or self there to transmigrate; it is the 'character' that transmigrates. In effect, what it means is that nothing of our thoughts and deeds disappear without leaving their mark behind, and that the 'good' and 'evil' so resulting recoil, not upon the doer (he is no more after death) but upon humankind (for the doer was never for a moment separate from humankind).

There are only thoughts; the self or the 'I' emerges by way of identifying itself (selectively) with thoughts, which in actuality do not solely belong to the self. It is like an individual getting hooked to a desire, depending upon his nature, and calling it his own.

The self is a continuity of thought and not a unity, and this process of continuity is the wheel of becoming, which is only another name for rebirth or reincarnation. Rebirth of thought feeling is a continuous process, not something that takes place at the end of one's life, but *now*, at every instant, with every breath. Just as you are reading this passage, the process of thinking going on inside of you is nothing but the self taking birth, and this is the continuity. If the continuity snaps even for a second, the thought structure collapses.

U.G. Krishnamurti says, 'Every thought that is born has to die. If a thought does not die, it cannot be reborn. It has to die, and with it you die. But you don't die with each thought and breath. You hook up each thought with the next, creating a false continuity.'[7]

The one who hooks up each thought with the next is the self. It is like a tree putting out a seed that produces another one like it; it is not the same tree but has all the characteristics of that tree. Similarity, therefore, should not be confused with sameness; continuity should not be confused with identity. It is in the nature of a tree to reproduce one like itself, so is the nature of the self to reproduce one like itself and that is rebirth, that is the perpetuation of samsara—the bhavachakra.

THOUGHT STRUCTURE

Samsara, the whole gamut of thought feeling, the whole collective or racial memory, is rooted in the 'I', like zillions of data in a chip; it is just one single thought at any given point of time and space, which is the self, which holds within it the whole collective consciousness. It is something like a negative of a picture of a person taken by using a laser beam. When you throw the negative on the ground and it breaks into several pieces, every little piece of the negative carries the complete picture of the person. Similarly, every little thought carries within it the collective consciousness, the thought structure.

What is being said here is that the collective memory is embedded in every single thought, which is the self, the coordinator of memory. And every time we are thought-feeling, we are giving momentum to this thought structure, the self. It is not going to stop. There is nothing we can do about it. All we can do is to understand or see how thought is taking birth and *that* is the reincarnation of the self, not actually taking birth again somewhere else.

So back to the question of rebirth. The answer is that it is the thought structure, the same thought structure we all have inherited, within which we play out our little lives, our stories of birth and death, joy and sorrow, fear and desire. And this thought structure has millions of years of momentum behind it.

However, for even a split second if the continuity of thought snaps, the primordial life force takes over. When the continuity of thought is broken, the body-mind undergoes the mutation that purifies or transforms the body-mind. Then, the body falls into a rhythm all its own and begins to express itself naturally and freely, while the self goes back to its *functional* role.

As I have explained earlier, the cessation of the continuity of this thought structure *is* nirvana. In one who has entered the state of nirvana, thoughts, instead of reproducing or replicating themselves, get burned, ionized, so to say. In the Buddha's words it is 'like a burnt seed which is no longer capable of sprouting'. Ramana Maharshi said, 'This apparent ego is harmless; it is like the skeleton of a burnt rope—though it has form, it is of no use to tie anything with.' Hence an enlightened person's mind is compared to a burnt seed or a burnt rope, and there is no rebirth and no continuity of the self for such a being. It simply means life has finished its play, fulfilled itself, achieved fruition. And this probably marks the end of evolution.

In the context of our discussion so far, let us now consider the prevalent belief in rebirth. Lately, the belief has gained a sort of quasi-scientific status. Stories of people remembering their past lives are cited to justify and prove the theory of reincarnation. It is said that there are well-researched cases of people remembering their past lives and that should prove beyond doubt that rebirth or reincarnation is the law of life. In the face of such 'formidable' research data it may sound strange and even rash to assert that all such accounts do not prove 'rebirth'; of course, nor can one disprove it either. It is a belief and the tremendous influence it has on our consciousness can create the 'reality'. That is to say, once we believe in a certain thing, it is possible to garner enough 'facts', enough data, to bolster the belief. And the power of thought can make things appear solid and true.

Now, we learn from the reports in medical sciences that even after a person stops breathing and is declared dead, the brain remains active for a while, that is, if the brain is not completely damaged or destroyed.[8] And from what U.G. Krishnamurti has said about dying and death—if we could hazard a theory—it takes about forty-five to forty-nine minutes for the brain to cease functioning completely. It is during this period perhaps, that the 'I', the hard disc, so to say, burns away. But, if and when the brain is completely damaged due to disease or injury, or for reasons we do not know, the personal hard disc, the emotional memories, the 'I', has no chance of burning away. It remains intact and is passed on to the pool of human consciousness, the server, if you like. And these (unburned) memories (still tied down to the earth, the place of its origin) probably get into some living individual mind and surface in flashes, as a memory of the past. How this happens nobody could tell. But this is only a theory or a probable fact, and cannot be proved on empirical/scientific grounds, just as we cannot prove that a particular individual's recall of certain events is really to do with events from a past life.

However, what is of critical importance for us to understand here is that the thought structure, the world mind, is something like a gigantic server and our individual mind, the self, is like a microchip, carrying within it the entire thought structure, which includes plant consciousness as well as animal consciousness.

U.G. Krishnamurti says that we have, through ideation, constructed a thought-feeling subject, our self, which we believe is ours, but which actually is a mere combination and permutation of the thoughts of other beings, of society. It is like picking a few colours from the seven basic colours found in nature and making a peculiar combination of our own, and this complex process is also probably influenced by heredity. But what exactly this complex process is, is not currently known to us; perhaps we will never know. In any case, it is basically the same or similar thought structure within each of us, where we play our little ego games and narrate our stories, though in actuality there is only one story. All our stories are like stories within stories within the immense and vast story of humankind.

Sunyata

Sunyata is usually translated into English as 'emptiness' or 'voidness'. The other terms used are 'openness', 'nothingness' and 'spaciousness'.

The doctrine of sunyata is central to the philosophy of Buddhism, especially of Madhyamika philosophy. But the exact definition of the notion of emptiness varies within the different Buddhist schools and this has often led to confusion. Indeed, the Pali canon and other Buddhist texts offer so many definitions and metaphors for the word that it becomes something like running through a dense forest looking for a lotus. And there are volumes written by monks and scholars, even doctoral theses, on the subject. Millions of words to describe and explain what cannot be verbalized, what cannot be framed in psychological terms!

Therefore, this whole effort to understand sunyata is going to be inevitably contradictory and in some way self-defeating. This was the dilemma of Nagarjuna, the second-century mystic, as well. But then, as the popular saying goes, 'If one has to philosophize, one has to philosophize; if one does not have to philosophize, one still has to philosophize.' So, since we have got into this telling and retelling affair, we cannot help but proceed, but bearing in mind Nagarjuna's warning that sunyata is 'a snake, which, if grasped at the wrong end, could be fatal'.

Now, Thervadins approach this subject cautiously, for emptiness is not something that can be understood intellectually; rather, it is a liberating insight that can be transmitted only when a student is ready. So they often use the terms 'impermanence' and 'selflessness' instead of 'emptiness'. For the Madhyamikas, however, it is a natural corollary of the teaching of conditioned genesis and the Middle Path, with profound epistemic implications.

All our knowledge is nothing but a compound of mutually dependent concepts and our experience a tantalizing play of these interdependent concepts, which, the Madhyamikas would assert, have no svabhava, essence, of their own. In other words, everything is conditioned, relative and interdependent. Nothing exists by itself or in itself. Therefore, to assume that all things and events are complete unto themselves or self-contained is a fundamental error. It is this error, or ignorance, that is the basis for attachment, clinging to pleasure, to views, to morality and external observances, and to belief in a soul or self. It is this attachment that sets off the wheel of becoming and the end result is dukkha.

There is nothing outside of the conditioned physical and mental elements that constitute our being. There is no higher reality; it is only a view that can neither be affirmed nor denied, and it is not about being true or false either. It is just that these concepts are not to be found. There is advaya, but to say there is one would imply there are two or more, therefore, to avoid such an ambiguity, such epistemological traps, Madhyamikas declare that reality, like nirvana, is sunya, empty, but this is not the opposite of something else.

However, religionists within the Buddhist fold considered such formulations, which would turn people away from The Way by a false impression of nihilism, as extreme negativism. Therefore, they (doesn't matter who or which school of thought; there are many) used positive language to describe not-self, sunyata and nirvana.

In the *Mahaparinirvana Sutra* (heavily influenced by the Thervadin school of thought) the Buddha himself is made to castigate those who view the Buddha nature as empty. Such a view of emptiness, goes the warning, does not conduce to the eradication of dukkha or enlightenment; instead, one will become 'like a moth in the flame of a lamp'.

Hence there is the affirmation that Buddhadhatu, nirvana, sunyata, point to a state of utter bliss, permanence. And the perfection of wisdom was interpreted as something not of not-self but the True Self. This eventually and naturally led to the elevation and adoration of Gautama Buddha as God, and offered a basis for the later Mahayana devotionalism. Perhaps the root of the bhakti tradition, which later spread rapidly among Hindus of various sects, where gods and then saints and sages were converted into deities, lies here.

However, these arguments and counter-arguments within and between different Buddhist schools are comparable to similar dialectics within the corpus of the Upanishads with regard to the notion of Atman-Brahman. Even within a single Upanishad, say, *Brihadaranyaka Upanishad*, we find Brahman described as neti, neti. On one hand, it is without attribute; on the other, it is described in positive terms—eternal bliss, Supreme Reality and so on.

NAGARJUNA

In his *Mulamadhyamaka Karika*, Nagarjuna shows a masterly approach to the problematic of sunyata and nirvana. He deploys the technique of four-corner negation to expose the limits of epistemology and demonstrate the futility of all attempts to know what cannot be known.

By drawing out the implications of the four alternative views that are possible on any subject, he shows their contradictory character. 'The dialectic is a series of *reductio ad absurdum* arguments (prasangapadanam). Every thesis is turned against itself.' Prasanga, disproof, writes T.R.V. Murti, 'is not to be understood as an apagogic proof in which we prove an assertion indirectly by disproving the opposite. Prasanga is a disproof simply, without the least intention to prove any thesis.[1]

In effect, all of this boils down to the question: when there is no thought, no self, who is to say reality is this or that, is or is not?

Nothing whatever arises. Not from itself, not from another, not from both itself and another, and not without a cause. (1.1)

If there are no existents, nor non-existents, nor existent non-existents, how can there be any causes? If there were a cause, what would it cause? (7.1)

It is all a dream, an illusion, like a city of the gods floating in the heavens. So much for arising, enduring, and dissolving. (7.34)

Liberation is the cessation of all thought, the dissolution of all plurality ... (25.24)

Do not say 'empty', or 'not empty', or both, or neither: these are mentioned for the sake of (conventional) understanding. (22.11)[2]

This negation of positions by Nagarjuna was not a position in itself, just as a criticism of theory is not necessarily another theory but can also be an awareness of the conditioned nature of all positions and views. Nagarjuna's statement was not a philosophical treatise aimed at challenging and destroying other views. It was meant to exhaust and reject all views as obstacles on the path to nirvana, which is no path at all. In other words, Nagarjuna's main concern was to demonstrate the fallacy of clinging to views, however profound or apparently valid, and to let go all our concepts and ideas, including the concept of sunyata and nirvana.[3]

Sunyata, therefore, is not a thesis or a theory but an art of *seeing*, where it empties everything, including itself.

The Nirguna poets, the poets of non-dualism, use oxymorons, negation and paradox in their poetry to express avyakta, the inexpressible, to hint at that which cannot be known. They do this by turning the language topsy-turvy and thus breaking rather than constructing ideas and images. Names and forms create illusions, yet they use names and forms to demolish them in order to give a sense of that which has no name and form. The twelfth-century sage Allama Prabhu is a classic example.

Allama was like a butterfly with no memory of the caterpillar, like space that goes naked. His vachanas, prose poems, are littered with explosive images and bewildering metaphors that always break and leap over and against the limitation and problematic of language. The mind is stunned reading about 'the toad that swallowed the sky', a 'black koel that eats up the sun' or the eye that turns within itself, seeing a 'blind man catch a snake'. Both the hunter and the hunted die and the seeker realizes that there is nothing to seek or to know because truth is neither here nor there, and the one who knows 'gets no results'. Here are some of his vachanas:

> Unless you burn fire, wet water,
> Unless you catch wind and conquer the sky,
> What can you know of the way of Yoga?

> The one who knows joy is not the happy one,
> the one who knows sorrow
> is not the unhappy one,
> the one who knows both joy and sorrow
> is not the jnani,
> only the one who grasps
> the sign of the dead and
> of the one who was never born,
> knows Lord Guhesvara.*

> If there is no desire,
> there is no imagination;
> if there is no imagination,
> there is no thinking;
> if there is no thinking,
> there is no Guheshvara;
> if there is no Guheshvara,
> there is no truth,
> no void, either.[4]

* Guhesvara: Lord of the caves

In our times, U. G. Krishnamurti's use of language may not have been as poetic but his use of words was explosive and startling, like the mind-boggling metaphors of Allama, and his method more akin to Nagarjuna's four-corner negation.

My interest is not to knock off what others have said, but to knock off what I am saying. More precisely, I am trying to stop what you are making out of what I am saying. This is why my talking sounds contradictory to others. I am forced by the nature of your listening to always negate the first statement with another statement. Then the second statement is negated by a third, and so on. My aim is not some comfy dialectical thesis, but the total negation of everything that can be expressed. Anything you try to make out of my statements is not it.[5]

EMPTINESS IS FULLNESS

Once, Ananda went to meet the Blessed One. Having bowed before him, he sat down near the Buddha. Then he asked him, 'It is said that the world is empty, the world is empty, lord. In what respect is it said that the world is empty?'

The Buddha said, 'Insofar as it is empty of a self or of anything pertaining to a self. Thus it is said, Ananda, that the world is empty. And what is empty of a self or of anything pertaining to a self? The eye is empty of a self or of anything pertaining to a self. Forms ... Eye-consciousness ... Eye-contact is empty of a self or of anything pertaining to a self.

The ear is empty ...
The nose is empty ...
The tongue is empty ...
The body is empty ...

The intellect is empty of a self or of anything pertaining to a self. Ideas ... Intellect-consciousness ... Intellect-contact is empty of a self or of anything pertaining to a self. Thus it is said that the world is empty.[6]

Thought brings in the thinker and creates the world. Thought, thinker and world are not different. Thought is sound, word, matter, and the word is the world. Without the word there is no world. It does not mean that the world, with its mountains and seas, flora and fauna and millions of living creatures, does not exist; instead, it is filtered through our binary mind, our divided consciousness. 'World' is an interpretation.

When the Buddha mentions the eye, ear, nose, tongue and body, he is referring to our sense experiences. All experiences are sense experiences, an interpretation of the world. Formations! With no formations taking place, the 'mind' is empty, not in the sense that there is no world but in the sense there is no thinker, no interpreter. Therefore, there are no formations, no experience at all.

Does it mean there is no pure sense experience? Yes and no. So long as the self is present there is no pure experience. The thinker uses the senses to frame or construct the world. He is the dictator who manipulates the senses to seek his continuity. This he does by dividing up the world as good and bad, pleasant and unpleasant, as opposites. This division is the dukkha. But it is not in the nature of the self, the ego, to let go of clinging and overcome dukkha. Only when the thought-feeling subject disappears, life is what it is and the senses operate independently. It is empty of all views. Then the eyes see things as they are and the body experiences the world as it is. This is what the Buddha means when he says that the eye, ear, nose, tongue, body are empty. This is Dhamma-cakkhu and yathabhutam.

Hence the Buddha's affirmation: 'Insofar as it is empty of a self or of anything pertaining to a self, the world is empty.'

We can understand this better in the light of what U.G. Krishnamurti says of sense experiences and the unitary movement of life:

The translation of sensations in terms of meaningful words is thought.

Every time thought takes its birth, you are giving life to that thought. You have translated the sensations in terms of a particular word, thereby you are giving continuity.

The body is responding to the various sensations. When sensations are bombarding the body all the time, senses are involved in looking, touching, smelling, tasting and hearing and what you do is you are all the time translating these senses in terms of your experiencing structure. You don't let the senses be.

This state [the natural state] is quite the opposite of what you think of the senses. Here the senses function at the peak of their capacity because the thinker, the interpreter of the senses, is not there.

When there is no 'I', no thinker or interpreter of the senses, what is there inside is complete, total emptiness; that emptiness is also fullness.[7]

Emptiness is also fullness and vice versa. The 'fullness' that the *Isavasya Upanishad* refers to is only another way of talking about sunyata, another way of expressing the state of nirvana, turiya or U.G. Krishnamurti's natural state, where the reality is not empty, but the mind is empty of all ideations. Life is what it is, and it cannot be comprehended in its totality in the fish bowl of the binary mind.

Silence! That silence is fullness, in the sense that everything exists there. What is there is there but it is also empty, by which I mean that there is no interpretation of what is there or what it is. All reference points have disappeared; in short, the binary mind has ceased to be. Full stop!

After this there are no words.

The Silence of the Buddha

Once, a wandering monk, Vacchagotta, came to the Buddha and asked, 'Tell me, venerable Gautama, is there the self?

The Buddha kept silent.

Vacchagotta asked again, 'How then, venerable Gautama, is there not the self?'

The Buddha still remained silent. And Vacchagotta rose from his seat and went away.

Ananda, who was there at the time, quite intrigued by the Buddha's silent response, asked, 'O Lord, how is that you didn't give an answer to the questions of Vacchagotta. I'm confused.'

The Buddha said,

Understand, Ananda, if I had said, yes, the self exists, then that would have confirmed the doctrine of the Samanas and Brahmanas who believe in permanence. And if I had said, no, the self does not exist, then that would have confirmed the doctrine of the Samanas and Brahmanas who believe in annihilation.[1]

This episode may be understood differently by different people depending upon their philosophical background. However, it brilliantly captures the dilemma involved in any teaching, and represents the distinctive style of the Buddha's teaching as well. We often go to a teacher not so much to seek answers to our questions as to seek a confirmation of the answers we already have. Therefore, a genuine teacher's response is based on the merit of the case. When a Buddha or a Ramana Maharshi or a U.G. Krishnamurti speaks or responds to a question, his utterances or silences are always in response to the context or to the particular situation or intention of the questioner.

Perhaps this is the way to understand the apparently different, sometimes contradictory answers a sage gives to the same questions. Take for instance Ramana Maharshi's answers to questions on rebirth or reincarnation. While he had answered the question in the affirmative, apparently giving credence to the idea of rebirth, there were occasions when he had responded to such questions by asking, 'Why do you want to know whether you existed in the past or are going to be reborn again? Are *you* there *now*, do *you* exist?'[2]

There will, of course, be elements in their utterances that may have a universal and enduring value, but many of their responses will be specific to the situation of the person asking the question and the context in which it is asked. This has to be understood because we have this blind belief that every act of a sage is holy, every utterance a 'revelation', and so we compile and systematize all their utterances and turn them into scriptures, believing them to be valid for all people and for all time. This is misleading, especially when it comes to the sage's response to social and political issues or situations.

All the same, every teaching of the sage, whether of the East or of the West, has to be examined, tested, validated and revalidated or rejected in the light of our experience. That is precisely what the Buddha meant when he said, 'Now, monks, are you going to say we respect the master and, out of respect for him, we believe this and that? You must not say so. Is not what you will say to be true, that exactly which you have by yourselves seen, known and apprehended?'[3]

Scriptures become problematic, even tyrannical, when, instead of furthering an open and honest endeavour of the intellect in its quest for knowledge and freedom, they offer 'fixed' truths in the name of God or 'revelation'. Once such fixed truths or beliefs are institutionalized and we create structures of spiritual or religious authority, there is no end to disputes, conflicts and power politics that corrupt our spiritual quest and turn religion into a fascist force. Over the centuries, we have seen that when religions or religious inquiry and practices are controlled and based on a book, we succeed only in producing bigotry, intolerance and irreconcilable conflicts and violence. Truth claims or a determinate truth invariably spell war and legitimize violence.

> One day, Sariputra went to the Blessed One, respectfully greeted him, sat down at one side, and spoke grandiloquently, 'This faith, Lord, I have in the Blessed One, that there has not been, there will not be, nor is there now, another recluse more exalted in Enlightenment than the Blessed One.'
>
> Surprised by Sariputra's presumptuous claim, the Buddha said, 'Lofty indeed is this speech of yours, Sariputra, and lordly! A bold utterance, a veritable sounding of the lion's roar! But how is this, Sariputra? Those Arahats, fully enlightened ones of the past, the future, and the present—do you have direct personal knowledge of all those blessed ones, as to their virtue, their meditation, their wisdom, their abiding, and their emancipation?'

'Not so, Lord.'

'Then it is clear, Sariputra, that you have no such direct personal knowledge of the Arahats, the fully enlightened ones of the past, the future, and the present. How then dare you set forth a speech so lofty and lordly, an utterance so bold?'[4]

We understand why the Buddha reprimands Sariputra. It is preposterous, even dangerous of a follower to claim, on behalf of a sage, exclusive possession of truth or insight into the mystery of life, when the sage himself makes no such claim. There is a lesson to be learnt here. No scripture, no master can make such a claim, for the Truth is that which should be available for everyone and at all times, provided of course one works for it and is prepared for it.

INDETERMINATE QUESTIONS

The Buddha's great silence with regard to fourteen metaphysical questions including the origin of the universe, the existence or otherwise of God and the Self, and the afterlife have led many to think that the Buddha was a nihilist, an agnostic or an atheist.

First we need to understand that these are our questions and our problems, not necessarily the Buddha's. He may not have had any doubt or confusion. It is not that the Buddha's attitude was just a suspension of judgement and that he was awaiting a more favourable time to reveal the truth. Nor was it the case that he had no reasoned conviction of the limits of knowledge, or that he had not arrived at clear conclusions on the truth of certain issues and therefore responded to certain questions with silence.[5]

There are all kinds of questions. Some can be answered directly; some questions require analysis before answer; others are answered by counter-questions. Then there are those that cannot be answered at all. The fourteen questions that were asked of him were of a metaphysical nature and he chose not to answer these questions simply because they cannot be answered. The Buddha characterized all such metaphysical questions or views as ditthigatanimani, matters of dogmatic speculation.

Once, determined to find answers to questions he considered fundamental to life, Vacchagotta asked the Buddha, 'Do you think the world is finite or infinite?

The Buddha said, 'I do not hold either of those views?'

'All right,' said Vacchagotta, 'then, do you believe that the soul and the body are the same, or that they are different?'

The Buddha replied that he held neither position. Vacchagotta, resolved to extract the Buddha's views, persisted with his questions. When the Buddha refused to answer his questions, Vacchagotta, quite exasperated, demanded if he held any view at all.

The Buddha said, 'To hold that the world is eternal or to hold that it is not, or to agree to any other of the propositions you adduce, Vaccha, is the jungle of theorising, the tangle of theorising, the bondage and shackles of theorising, attended by distress, perturbation and fever; it conduces not to detachment, tranquillity, peace, to knowledge and wisdom of nirvana. This is the danger I perceive in these views, which makes me discard them all.

'The Tathagata, O Vaccha, is free from all theories; but this, Vaccha, does the Tathagata know—the nature of form, and how form arises, and how form perishes; the nature of sensation, and how sensation arises, and how sensation perishes; the nature of perception, and how perception arises, and how perception perishes; the nature of the predispositions, and how the predispositions arise, and how the predispositions perish; the nature of consciousness, and how consciousness arises, and how consciousness perishes. Therefore, say I that the Tathagata has attained deliverance and is free from attachment, inasmuch as all imaginings, or agitations, or proud thoughts concerning an Ego or anything pertaining to an Ego, have perished, have faded away, have ceased, have been given up and relinquished.'[6]

Questions are evidence of the conflict or doubt in our knowledge system. So, approaching the issue from a different angle, U.G. Krishnamurti would say that it is not the questions but the answers that are the problem here. This is because the old answers are not satisfactory or convincing, because they cause more confusion and thereby give rise to more questions. And we keep asking questions, hoping one day we will find the right answers.

The truth is that all our questions with regard to the origin of things, God, love, life after death, the soul and so on are all only variations of one theme: our search for a centre, for permanence, which does not exist. Questions such as 'What is God?', 'Who or what am I?', 'What is the purpose and meaning of life?', 'What is love?', 'How did the universe come into existence?', 'Is there life after death?' and so on are all questions that arise from the concepts and ideas or answers we have already been given by culture/tradition/gurus, and since they don't work—well, we are not too sure they are the right answers—we find ourselves in a quandary.

In actuality, there are no questions (except in the technical field, although they are relative and related), there are only unsatisfactory or unconvincing answers (gathered over centuries). From these answers we create questions, much like the way problems are created out of solutions in mathematics.

❧

Once, a man called Malunkyaputta approached the Buddha with a series of metaphysical questions.

> The Buddha asked, 'Why do you wish to know these things?
>
> Malunkyaputta said, 'Without knowing the answers to these questions what is the point of following you?'
>
> The Buddha said, 'You are like a man who has been struck by a poisoned arrow. Your friends take you to the healer so that the arrow can be removed and an antidote given for the poison. But you refuse to allow the healer to remove the arrow until he first answers all your questions. Who shot the arrow at you? What was his motive? What kind of arrow is it? What kind of poison did he use? On and on you ask such questions while the arrow remains in your body with the poison seeping into your blood and you die before your questions are answered.
>
> I have not answered the questions such as the ones you have asked because they do not conduce to an absence of passion, to tranquility and nirvana. And what have I explained? Suffering have I explained, the cause of suffering, the destruction of suffering, and the path that leads to the destruction of suffering have I explained. For this is useful.[7]

The primary task, therefore, is to end sorrow. Once the sorrow ends there are only practical questions such as how to go from Bengaluru to Mysuru, where is the milk, where are you from, how to operate a cellphone and so on. All other questions, especially the metaphysical questions, will have disappeared because we will have understood that there are no answers to such questions. In other words, the self is the question and the questioner, the answer and the answerer. The self is forever caught in the wheel of becoming, and once this self disappears or is put in its right place, all metaphysical questions disappear along with it.

BOOK THREE

Mahasamadhi

The Final Absorption

Mahaparinirvana

Perhaps the last days of the Buddha do read like a depressing tale. But the account of the Buddha going away from the city to breathe his last in a remote village sounds like the final sutra calling for deep contemplation on the nature of life and how to come to terms with it.

Much as we expect a happy end in books and movies, we wish and even expect that the life of a sage should end on a high and glorious note, better still if there is a supernatural touch to it. The fact of the matter, however, is contrary to our self-indulgent expectation. As a rule, it seems, the way the sages pass away subverts our grand narratives. The problem here is not with the sages or the way they die, but in us, in our false hopes. There is nothing mysterious or unnatural in the way, say, the Buddha, Sri Ramakrishna, Ramana Maharshi or U.G. Krishnamurti passed away, not to speak of Jesus Christ's crucifixion. It seems that in their death they preside over a destruction that is necessary for recreation, for a new beginning. Seeds are sown but how the seeds will sprout and blossom into a tree cannot be foreseen or predicted.

LAST DAYS

During the last days of the Buddha, the world is not exactly falling apart but the old system has started to crumble. The king of Kosala, Pasenedi, an old friend and admirer of the Buddha, troubled and seeking peace, meets with him. It is a moving story: an eighty-year-old king meeting with an eighty-year-old sage. But the meeting does no good for the old king. His own son, Prince Vidudabha, takes control of the kingdom in his absence and drives his father out. Abandoned, with no help coming from any quarter, he falls seriously ill and dies a 'disgraceful' death. While in the powerful neighbouring kingdom, Magadha, Prince Ajatashatru throws his father, King Bimbisara (another dear friend and admirer of the Buddha), into prison and starves him to death.

Suddenly, it seems like a world where the Buddha has never walked and taught the Four Noble Truths and loving kindness to all forms of life. Egotism, hatred and greed, the unskilful passions he has warned against, seem to reign supreme. Legend says (as if to mitigate the damage) that the Buddha, even without direct intervention, prevents Ajjatasatta from warring against the Vajjians. However, the peace lasts for a short period and soon, through devious means, Ajjatasatta defeats the Vajjians. To make matters even worse, shortly after the Buddha leaves Rajagriha, Vidudabha defeats and massacres the Buddha's own clan, the Sakyas, sparing neither children nor women.

As if the political upheaval and bloody massacre were not bad enough, there is a schism within the sangha. Devadatta, the Buddha's brother-in-law, who had entered the sangha after the Buddha's first visit to Kapilavastu, rebels against the Buddha and tries to seize control over the sangha. 'The Blessed One is now old and has reached the last stage of his life,' argues Devadatta. 'Let him now rest and give up the sangha to me.' Charging the Buddha with going soft on the discipline of the sangha and letting 'corruption' set in, he proposes five new rules for the monks.

There is enough evidence in the Pali texts to show that the Buddha was not the leader of the sangha and he exercised no authority over the monks, though he did talk to them freely and openly. It was entirely the lot and responsibility of the monks to take care of themselves and each other, and diligently and skilfully pursue their goal. However, the Buddha could not allow Devadatta to sow the seeds of dissent and break the community of monks.

So the Buddha was left with no alternative but to publicly disassociate himself from Devadatta. Devadatta grew desperate and plotted to kill the Buddha but failed in the attempt. Soon after, he committed suicide, though there is another version of the story that says he died of illness before he was able to be reconciled with the Buddha.

With the world thus crumbling around him, the Buddha decided to leave Rajagriha. He had spent the greater part of his life in Magadha and Kosala, moving around and teaching in cities such as Rajagriha, Kosambi, Sravasti and Varanasi. That work was at an end now; he was finished with teaching.

It is interesting to note here that travelling north, the Buddha touched about fourteen different places before proceeding to the distant village of the Mallas in Kusinara (modern Kushinagar, Uttar Pradesh). It was as if he was bidding farewell to the people he knew before he went to die in an utterly strange place among unknown people.

The Pali canon says that with a large entourage of monks, the Buddha and Ananda journeyed through Magadhan territory, going first to Nalanda. From Nalanda, passing through three different villages, they went to Vesali one last time.

At Vesali, Ambapali, a wealthy and famous courtesan, invites him to a meal and donates her mango grove to the sangha. The Buddha does not stay there for long. He speaks to the monks about the way of the Dhamma and then tells them not to follow him thereafter.

> Go now, monks, and seek shelter anywhere in the neighbourhood of Vesali where you are welcome, among acquaintances and friends, and there spend the rainy season. As for me, I shall spend the rainy season in the village of Beluva.[1]

And to Beluva he goes with only Ananda as his companion. Just as monsoon rains begin, the Buddha falls seriously ill. From here on, with all the monks including the ones who were a part of the inner circle gone, the Buddha and Ananda have to take care of themselves, a fact the canon disguises.

Alone with the Buddha, now sick and very weak, Ananda realizes for the first time that his master could die soon. Overcome with fear and anxiety, he asks what will happen to the sangha after he has gone. The Buddha responds thus:

> What more does the community of bhikkhus expect from me, Ananda? I have preached the truth without making any distinction between exoteric and esoteric doctrine; for in respect of the truths, Ananda, the Tathagata has no such thing as the closed fist of a teacher, who keeps some things back.
>
> Surely, Ananda, should there be any one who harbours the thought, 'It is I who will lead the brotherhood,' or, 'The Order is dependent upon me,' it is he who should lay down instructions in any matter concerning the Order. Now the Tathagata, Ananda, thinks not that it is he who should lead the brotherhood, or that the Order is dependent upon him. Why

then should he leave instructions in any matter concerning the Order? ...

O Ananda, be you lamps unto yourselves. Be you a refuge to yourselves. Seek no external refuge. Hold fast to the Truth as a lamp. Hold fast as a refuge to the Truth. Look not for refuge to any one besides yourselves.[2]

It is obvious the Buddha never saw himself as head of the sangha. And during his time, there is enough indication to believe that the sangha had not been institutionalized. Only after his death, *Vinaya Pitaka*, the canon with regard to the rules and discipline of the sangha, was gradually developed, and the third of the Three Refuges 'sangham saranam' was added to the other two refuges: 'Buddham saranam' and 'dhammam saranam gacchami'.

Returning to the last days of the Buddha, two more significant things happened at Beluva. The Buddha and Ananda came to know of the death of their senior monks, Sariputra and Moggallana, at the hands of a band of robbers in Nalanda. The text does not go into the details of these two sudden deaths. While the Buddha received the news calmly, as if he knew it beforehand, Ananda fell into a depression. The Buddha asked him, 'What did you expect, Ananda? Don't you know nothing lasts forever and that one day or the other we lose everything and everybody we love? Why are you in such distress, Ananda? Is it that you imagine that Sariputra has taken with him the laws and insights by which monks live, or that the code of virtue and the knowledge of meditation has departed from the sangha?'[3]

MARA: LET GO

Then the Pali text, *Mahaparinirvana Sutra*, brings in Mara to round up the narrative. Mara is now no more a fierce demon or the power of passion; rather, he speaks like a friend, gently reminding the Buddha of his word. Not surprisingly, Mara's words sound like a thought that emerges from the depth of the Buddha's own consciousness.

> 'Pass away now, Lord; let the Exalted One now die. Now is the time for the Exalted One to pass away ...'
>
> The Exalted One said, 'Make thyself happy, Mara, the death of the Tathagata shall take place before long. At the end of three months from this time the Tathagata will pass away.'[4]

At the Chapala shrine in Vesali, the Pali text states that the Buddha 'deliberately and consciously abandoned the will to live.' He was eighty years old and had become weak and delicate. The life had been lived, what had to be done had been done and it was time to go. It was not so much a conscious decision to die as to let go of things. For the Buddhas know when it is time to go and they go. The tradition, however, believes that if only Ananda had asked the Buddha not to die, 'to live on for the good and happiness of the great multitudes, out of compassion for the world,' the Buddha would have prolonged his life. The text even makes the Buddha speak to that effect! But the great masters don't decide either to live or die; it is not a matter of choice.

DEATH PANGS

After recovering from his illness, the Buddha and Ananda slowly journeyed north through six different villages before they reach Pava. In Pava, the death pangs began.

While residing in Pava, Chunda, 'a metal worker', invited the Buddha for a meal. Chunda was probably a prominent person in Pava and perhaps he wished the holy man to bless his family by having a meal at his place. Nobody is quite sure what dish Chunda served the Buddha. The Pali canon uses the term 'sukaramaddava'. Scholars more or less agree that 'sukara' refers to a pig and 'maddava' means soft and tender, indicating a dish made of the tender parts of a pig or boar. However, there are also scholars who believe that the term refers to a mushroom, yam or tuber.[5]

The Buddha couldn't have possibly declined such an offer made with affection. Going by the texts, he never ate meat. That day, perhaps he did not know it was meat or he did not want to decline the offer or, they were actually just wild mushrooms he ate. Whatever the fact is, it is secondary. It is emotions like hatred, envy, anger, egotism and greed that constitute uncleanliness, not the eating of flesh. That is to say, 'It is not that which entereth into man that defileth him, but that which comes out.'[6] Or, as U. G. Krishnamurti would say, 'Vegetarianism has nothing to do with spirituality. What you put in there [the stomach] is not really the problem.'[7]

The *Mahaprinirvana Sutra* recounts that the Buddha, having eaten some portion of the dish, asked Chunda not to serve it to anyone else and to bury what was left in a pit, since nobody would be able to digest it and survive. The implication here could be that the Buddha knew that the dish had been laced with poison. We do not know for sure and it's hard to imagine the real reason. Later, the Buddha is believed to have told Ananda that Chunda was not to be blamed for his death and he should make that clear when the time comes.

However, it appears that the dish aggravated the Buddha's already weak condition. That night he vomited blood and suffered from dysentery and gripping pain. But soon, as the text would have it, he recovered. We are also told that Subhadda, a former disciple of Alara Kalama, sought the Buddha's refuge and was made his last disciple.

The Buddha's health remained poor. It is quite likely that during his last days, he stopped consuming food and let the body burn itself out. One day, unable to bear the sight of his master reduced to skin and bones, Ananda wept. He was in agony because he knew the master was dying, and also because even after having followed and lived with the master for many years, he had come nowhere near attaining the perfection of wisdom.

FAREWELL

The Buddha sends for Ananda and gently admonishes him thus:

> Enough, Ananda! Do not grieve, do not lament! For have I not taught from the very beginning that with all that is dear and beloved there must be change, separation and severance? Of that which is born, come into being, compounded and subject to decay, how can one say: 'May it not come to dissolution'? There can be no such state of things. Now for a long time, Ananda, you have served the Tathagata with loving-kindness in deed, word and thought, graciously, pleasantly, with a whole heart and beyond measure. Great good have you gathered, Ananda! Now you should put forth energy, and soon you too will be free from ignorance and delusion.[8]

Then the Buddha tells him to spread a sheet under the sal tree so that he can lie down. Realizing the final moment has come, Ananda, tears running down his face, asks, 'What are we to do, Lord, with the remains of the Tathagata?'

The Pali canon holds that the Buddha instructs Ananda thus: 'As men treated the remains of a chakravarthi, king of kings, so should they treat the remains of Tathagata.' The text also says that the Mallas of Kusinara organize the funeral and the venerable Mahakasyapa, a senior monk, promptly appears to light the pyre, which, strangely, could not be hitherto lit by anybody else. Then, the representatives from the king of Magadha, the Licchavis of Vesali, the Sakyas of Kapilavastu, the Mallas of Pava, the Bulis of Allakappa, the Koliyas of Ramagama and the Brahmins of Vethadipa arrive to claim the relics.

This gathering of royal representatives at the Buddha's funeral is highly unlikely because, before the Buddha dies, Ananda begs him not to die unattended, unsung and abandoned in a place like Kusinara, cut off from the 'civilized world'.

> Let it not be, Lord, that the Blessed One should pass away in this mean place, this uncivilized township in the midst of the jungle, a mere outpost of the province. There are great cities, Lord, such as Champa, Rajagriha, Savatthi, Saketa, Kosambi, and Benares—let the Blessed One have his final passing away in one of those. For in those cities dwell many wealthy nobles and brahmins and householders who are devotees of the Tathagata, and they will render due honour to the remains of the Tathagata.[9]

If the Buddha wanted his body to be treated like the remains of a chakravarti, it is doubtful that he would have decided to leave the city and die in a remote place like Kusinara. It is most likely that the Buddha would have said words to this effect: 'Ananda, how is that you still don't understand. Whether one dies in Rajagriha or Kusinara, what difference does it make for the one who is no more? Everything that lives has to pass away one day and yet nothing goes away completely. Everything returns, everything exists. All existence is one. So, Ananda, what does it matter where the Buddha dies?'

ONENESS

Rhys Davids writes, 'Gautama was born and brought up and lived and died a Hindu.'[10] This is a questionable view, coming from a great scholar and translator. It is tantamount to listening to the story of Ramayana the whole night and the next day morning asking the question: What is the relationship between Rama and Sita?

The Buddha did not die a Hindu or a Buddhist. But then, who or what is a Hindu or a Buddhist? A name, a form, a set of beliefs and practices, a state of mind? They are just mental formations! They are like 'impurities' for a Dharmakaya, for the one who is in an undivided state of consciousness.

A Buddha is not a Buddhist, he has no religious identity. A Buddha or a Tathagata is one who is free from measure and form (rupa-sankha-vimutto), deep and unfathomable like the ocean, beyond predication. This is the state of Freedom, beyond boundaries and borders, in living as in death, which is no death.

If nirvana is the 'blowing out' of all 'mentations' or 'ideations' and the cooling of the passion of the body, which then falls into a rhythm all its own and is in tune with the cosmos, mahaparinirvana is the final burning away of whatever traces have been left since nirvana. It is the final extinction, in which even the (bodily) will to live or the survival instinct (which drives all life forms to eat and avoid danger), is extinguished, and so completely extinguished that there is no difference between the body of the Buddha and the sun, a rock or tree. That is the Oneness that is always already there, at the beginning and at the end, which is no end but a movement of life with no direction, no beginning and no end ...

The Way

For nearly 500 years after the Buddha's death, paintings and carvings in wood and stone depicted the Bodhi tree or the emblem of the Wheel (of dhamma) in Buddhist viharas, symbolizing nirvana. But there were no images of the Buddha.[1] For, Siddhartha Gautama, upon coming into the state of nirvana, had disappeared.

Only later, for reasons not beyond our understanding, the image of the Buddha began to be portrayed and the Bodhi tree became a blur in the background, or totally disappeared. As years passed, statues of the Buddha in all sizes, some of them imposingly, monstrously tall, started to appear in every part of the world, even in 'secular' spaces, not to speak of monasteries and temples. In modern times, the image makers, with their wizardry of mass production, have made figurines of the Buddha in wood, stone and metal for mass consumption. The Buddha is even a part of the decor in homes and offices today. Iqbal Singh puts it well when he writes,

> The Face of Silence can at last be seen in practically every curiosity shop east as well as west of Greenwich; serene,

detached, slightly cynical and world-weary; it seems to watch the mad rush of this age with a baffling indifference … Had Gautama himself seen all this, perhaps he would have enjoyed the joke.[2]

For nearly three centuries after the first turning of the Wheel of Law, the way of the Buddha had remained predominantly a spiritual sect, with scores of monasteries spread across the Gangetic plain. It is a historical fact that all major religions spread across the world largely because of royal patronage and proselytization, otherwise they would have remained as sects or cults. So it happened with the way of the Buddha too.

After the third council (c. 250 BCE) under the patronage of King Ashoka (c. 268–232 BC), the teachings of the Buddha grew into a full-fledged religion and started to spread across the world, but at a price. Compromises were made at the cost of losing its originality, and through the back door, many beliefs and practices that the Buddha had denied having any spiritual significance were introduced. Joseph Campbell writes, 'In the Rock Edicts of Ashoka, which are the earliest Buddhist writings we possess, no mention whatsoever is made of the doctrine of no-self, ignorance and extinction, but only of heaven, good works, merit and the soul.'[3]

And the way of the Buddha began to be predominantly interpreted in terms of 'performance' or 'engagement' with society rather than 'cessation' and 'disengagement'. It was this shift, from an apparently negative approach to a 'liberal' and positive approach, along with the portrayal of the Buddha as the Compassionate One, preaching the dhamma as the way to end suffering, that was instrumental in spreading Buddhism all over the world.

In the face of this historical shift and the fact that there are today several million Buddhists in China, Japan, Cambodia,

Indonesia and Sri Lanka, following several different cults or traditions, it would sound ridiculous to say that the way of the Buddha is not a religion. It certainly is a religion but with a difference: it is not a historical revelation or a covenant but a yana, a way or a vehicle, to be undertaken by an individual with no external aid to reach the shore of nirvana. As Sri Rahula says, it does not matter what name we give to this journey: 'Buddhism remains what it is whatever label you may put on it. The name one gives it is inessential.'[4]

YANA

It is indeed a yana, a journey in search of truth. Gautama's search and sadhana for truth, it will be recalled, was not something new. The sramana and sanyasa traditions, especially the Upanishadic traditions and the existence of several schools of thought much before Gautama would begin his journey, show that he walked a familiar path. But the way he did the search, with such great rigour, intelligence and honesty, and the breakthrough he achieved were something utterly new and revolutionary.

There is no God or Absolute, no model of perfection, no soul or paradise, because they do not exist; rather, they exist only in the mind. They are projections of our fears and desires, inventions of an insecure mind in search of permanence. God is a relief, solace, an anchor we seek against an apparently chaotic world. It is comfortable to believe that there is a supreme power out there that has created us and the universe, and that that power, like a father figure, will take care of us, provided of course we surrender to Him.

Such a God, created in our own image, with likes and dislikes similar to our own, writes Karen Armstrong:

... it is all too easy to make 'him' endorse some of our most uncharitable, selfish and lethal hopes, fears and prejudices. This limited God has thus contributed to some of the worst religious atrocities in history. The Buddha would have described belief in a deity who gives a seal of sacred approval to our own selves as 'unskillful'. This could only embed the believer in the damaging and dangerous egotism that he or she was supposed to transcend.[5]

The Buddha was merciless. He did not bring the dead back to life but taught us to reckon with death as a fact of life and not to escape into beliefs that have no basis in reality. He refused to offer false promises, props or sugar-coated pills to comfort us or allow us any childish desires. He would not allow us to cling to any lie, howsoever consoling, for a lie is a lie and it can only produce false consciousness and thereby conflict and sorrow. The truth has to be brought to us, no matter how hard and unpalatable it is.

There are any number of passages in the texts that show Brahmans, sramanas and seekers, belonging to different schools of thought, getting shocked by the Buddha's response to their questions on karma, soul, liberation, the nature of consciousness and so on. What the Buddha offered was not a new set of beliefs in the place of old ones but a radically new way of seeing that entailed dropping their beliefs, their old habits of being and doing things in the world.

In other words, the Buddha, like U.G. Krishnamurti in our times, offered the possibility of freedom from the tyranny of gods, from the authority of the Word, from illusory goals. And once we are courageous enough to see the truth of it all, we realize that there is compassion in such a teaching; it is a benediction.

All religions claim that their scriptures are not man-made but of divine origin, a revelation fixed for all time, and unquestionable. This belief serves well the pontiffs and gurus, bolstering their spiritual authority. And this belief can succeed only by suppressing rather than encouraging free and open inquiry into the human condition, in creating pointless controversy, intolerance and violence. Needless to say that some of the greatest crimes against humanity have been committed not only in the name of science and nation or some political ideology, but also in the name of God and Book.

The Buddha does not ask us to believe him or in his words but to doubt, to question not only his words but even our own pet beliefs and experiences. He asks us not to accept an idea just because it is given in the scriptures or uttered by gurus, or is a popular and appealing belief.

This was the wisdom the Buddha shared with the Kalamas. Many practising Buddhists would agree that the Buddha advised the Kalamas to find things out for themselves, to find skilful thoughts and actions that promoted compassion and a healthy and intelligent way of living, that would finally take them towards enlightenment.

But these practitioners would insist that the Buddha did not rule out the importance of faith. By faith they meant faith in the Buddha, that he was a fully enlightened master and therefore could show the way, his words leading one to the other shore. This is understandable, for that is how a religion develops and spreads among people who need an anchor.

However, though we may not go with such a belief in the Buddha and be willing to see him as God, we may yet agree here that the life of the Buddha certainly assures us that nirvana is possible, for he was a living example of that freedom in action. His words can give us that impetus, that much-required nudge we need to become alert, to become mindful of things as they are, to never compromise and to be ruthlessly honest with ourselves so we can finally come upon wisdom.

In this context, we may think of the fiery words of the great ninth-century spiritual master of China, Rinzai Gigen, who declared, 'I have no dharma to give ... There is no Buddha, no dharma, no training and no realization ... If you meet the Buddha on the road, kill him!'

In a way, his harsh words capture the core of the Buddha's teaching: 'Form is not yours, give it up. Sensation, perception, the formation and consciousness are not yours. Give them up.'[6]

Give up the Buddha too, for you are not him. Each one is unique, unparalleled. Tread your own path, be diligent and be vigilant. Nirvana is not an achievement, you cannot go to it; it has to come to you and it comes when you drop everything, when you lose all your ideas, your ego, the body—everything. Then you shall be a light unto yourself.

The long passage quoted below is from Hsi Yun, one of the Ch'an (Zen) masters who lived about AD 840. While this brilliantly captures the way of the Buddha, this should also serve as a fitting finale to this reflective narrative:

> One day the Buddha called Kasyapa and said to him that there is a way, but wherever there is division into this or that, that is not the way, and there is no truth; and then he added, *when a silent understanding of it is obtained, you enter the state of nirvana* [italics mine].
>
> Kasyapa asked: 'What is the Way and what must one do to follow it?'
>
> The Buddha said: 'Is then the Way something objective? For that is what your wish to follow it implies.'
>
> Kasyapa: 'What are the instructions for practising dhyana and studying the Way which has been transmitted by all the various teachers?'

The Buddha: 'Words that are used to attract the dull-witted should not be relied upon.'

Kasyapa: 'If these teachings are meant to attract the dull-witted, I have not heard the Dharma, which is intended for people of the highest capacity.'

The Buddha: 'If they are really people of the highest capacity, where can they find others to be followed? If they seek from within themselves they will still find nothing tangible. How much less can they do so from elsewhere? You should not look to what, in instructing others, is called the Dharma, for what Dharma could that be?'

Kasyapa: 'Then we should not seek for anything at all?'

The Buddha: 'By conceding this you would save yourself a lot of mental effort.'

Kasyapa: 'But in this way everything would be eliminated. There cannot be just nothing.'

The Buddha: 'Who teaches that there is nothing? What is this nothing? But you implied you wanted to seek for something.'

Kasyapa: 'Since there is no need to seek, why do you also say that we should not eliminate everything?'

The Buddha: 'If you do not seek, that is enough. Who told you to eliminate anything? Observe the Void which lies before your eyes. How can you set about eliminating it?'

Kasyapa: 'If I can reach this Dharma, will it prove to be like the Void?'

The Buddha: 'When have I said to you of the Void that is like or unlike something? I spoke in that way as a temporary expedient, but you are reasoning literally from it.'

Kasyapa: 'Do you mean, then, that one should not reason so?'

The Buddha: 'I have not prevented you, but reasoning is related to attachment. When attachment arises, wisdom is shut out.'

Kasyapa: 'Should we, then, not allow any attachment to arise from it [in the search for the Dharma]?'

The Buddha: 'If attachment does not arise, who can say what is right or wrong?'

Kasyapa: 'When I spoke to your Reverence, just now, in what way was I mistaken?'

The Buddha: 'You are one who does not understand what is said. What is this about being mistaken?'

Kasyapa: 'Up to now, everything you have said has been in the nature of refutation, but none of it contains any guidance as to what is the true Dharma.'

The Buddha: 'The true Dharma contains no confusion but by implying such a question you make confusion for yourself. What is this "true Dharma" you seek?'

Kasyapa: 'Since I have given rise to confusion by my question, what is your answer to my problem?'

The Buddha: 'Observe things as they are and do not worry about other people ... Since the doctrine was first transmitted, it has never been taught that people should seek knowledge or look for explanations of things. We merely talk about "studying the Way" using the phrase as a term to arouse people's interest. In fact, the Way cannot be studied. If concepts based on study are retained, they only result in the Way being misunderstood.'

Kasyapa: 'Since there is nothing on which to lay hold, how should the Dharma be transmitted?'

The Buddha: 'It is transmitted from mind to mind.'

Kasyapa: 'If mind is used for this purpose, how can it be said that mind does not exist?'

The Buddha: 'Obtaining absolutely nothing is called receiving transmission from mind to mind.'

Kasyapa: 'If there is no mind and no Dharma, what is meant by "transmission"?'

The Buddha: 'It is because you people on hearing of transmission from mind to mind, take it to mean that there is something to be obtained ... It is because you are not capable of this [the elimination of analytic thinking—mentation] that you feel the necessity of using the mind to study Dhyana and study the Way. How will the Dharma be able to help you?

'All that was spoken by the Tathagata was for the purpose of influencing men. It was like using yellow leaves for gold to stop the crying child, and was decidedly not real. If you take it for something real, what relation can it have to your real self?

'In reality there is not the smallest thing which can be grasped is called supreme, perfect wisdom. If you can understand this, you will see the Way of the Buddhas.

'Everything is pure and glistening, neither square nor round, big nor small, long nor short; it is beyond passion and phenomena, ignorance and Enlightenment.'

Then finally, stepping into the public hall, the Buddha declared: 'The knowledge of many things cannot compare for the excellence with giving up the search. The sage is one who puts himself outside the range of objectivity. There are not different kinds of mind, and there is no doctrine which can be taught.'

As there was no more to be said, everybody went away ...[7]

Notes and References

Introduction

1.	Karen Armstrong, *Buddha*, London: Phoenix, 2006.
2.	Sangharakshita, *A Survey of Buddhism: Its Doctrines and Methods through the Ages*, London: Tharpa Publications, 1987.
3.	Ibid.
4.	Hermann Oldenberg, *Buddha: His Life, His Doctrine, His Order*, translated from the German by William Hoey, London: Williams and Norgate, 1882.
5.	M. Hiriyanna, *Outlines of Indian Philosophy*, Bombay: George Allen & Unwin, 1973.
6.	*Majjhima Nikaya* I. 134. Pali Text Society, Translated from the Pali by Thanissaro Bhikkhu; www.accesstoinsight.org (accessed on 22 March 2017).

BOOK ONE
TATHAGATA: ONE WHO HAS THUS GONE

Going Forth

1.	For Gautama's historical background see Hermann Goldberg, Joseph Campbell and Karen Armstrong.

2. Edwin Arnold, *The Light of Asia and the Indian Song of Songs*, Calcutta: Jaico Publishing House, 1949.

3. In the Pali canon, this state of consciousness is called the first jhana and the description of this experience may not resemble the near-death experience of, say, either Ramana Maharshi or U.G. Krishnamurti. Descriptions could be misleading, but we understand it was the life-altering 'near-death experience'.

4. Arthur Osborne, *Ramana Maharshi and the Path of Self-knowledge*, Tiruvannamalai: Sri Ramanasramam, 1970; also see, Mukunda Rao, *The Other Side of Belief: Interpreting U.G. Krishnamurti*, New Delhi: Penguin India, 2005.

The End of the Search

1. Hermann Oldenberg, *Buddha: His Life, His Doctrine, His Order*, translated from the German by William Hoey, London: Williams and Norgate, 1882.

2. Friedrich Nietzsche, *Twilight of the Idols and The Antichrist*, trans. by Thomas Common, New York: Dover Publications, Inc., 2004.

3. Karen Armstrong, *Buddha*, London: Phoenix, 2006.

4. Ibid.

5. S. Radhakrishnan, *Indian Philosophy*, Vol. 1, New Delhi: Oxford University Press, 1989.

6. There seems to be a strange pattern in the manner of the appearance of sages. They appear in twos, like some form of dialectics within the culture, or as a form of complementarities. To mention a few, take the cases of Socrates and Plato, Jesus and John the Baptist, Buddha and Mahavira, U.G. Krishnamurti and J. Krishnamurti, Ramana Maharshi and Nisargadata Maharaj, Sri Ramakrishna and Vivekananda.

7. The Pali texts do not mention any meeting between the Buddha and Mahavira. But they do refer to Mahavira as Niggantha Nataputta, the liberated one. Further, *Anguttara Nikaya* quotes the philosopher Purana Kasyapa (the sixth-century founder of a

now extinct order) as listing the Nirgranthas, Jains, as one of the six major classifications of humanity.

8. S. Radhakrishnan, *Indian Philosophy*, Vol. 1.

9. Ibid.

10. The twin concepts such as Purusha-Prakriti, yin-yang, jiva-ajiva and jiva-ishvara, representing the idea of active and passive, motion and stillness, have a biological basis, like the concept of male and female. It is to construct a philosophy of *balance*, where two opposites coexist in harmony and are able to transmute into each other. Feminists may argue that such a philosophy/metaphysics of dualism (wherein the male principle was privileged) has been instrumental in developing patriarchy.

11. Rodney Arms (ed.), *The Mystique of Enlightenment: The Unrational Ideas of a Man called U.G.*, Goa: Dinesh Vaghela, 1982.

12. *Majjhima Nikaya* 66.

13. Ibid.

14. Where Swami Prabhavananda translates 'ajnana' or ignorance as 'body', which makes sense, many translators of the Upanishads, for instance, Swami Nikhilananda, translate 'ajnana' as 'ignorance' or 'rituals'.

> Into a blind darkness they enter who are devoted to ignorance; but into a greater darkness they enter who engage in knowledge of a deity alone.
> He who is aware that both knowledge and ignorance should be pursued together, overcomes death through ignorance and obtains immortality through knowledge.
> *Isavasya Upanishad* 9, 11, 12. From *The Upanishad*, a new translation by Swami Nikhilananda, Calcutta: Ramakrishna Ashram, 2006.

15. Karen Armstrong, *Buddha*.

16. Mukunda Rao (ed.), *The Biology of Enlightenment: Unpublished Conversations of U.G. Krishnamurti after He Came into the Natural State (1967-71)*, Noida, India: HarperCollins, 2010.

17. *Majjhima Nikaya* 36.

18. Thich Nhat Hanh, *Old Path White Clouds: Walking in the Footsteps of the Buddha*, New Delhi: Full Circle, India, 2007.

19. Karen Armstrong, *Buddha*.

20. *Majjhima Nikaya* 66.

Nirvana

1. *Majjhima Nikaya* 36. Also see *Samyutta Nikaya* 12:65.

2. Mukunda Rao (ed.), *The Biology of Enlightenment: Unpublished Conversations of U.G. Krishnamurti after He Came into the Natural State (1967–71)*, Noida, India: HarperCollins, 2010.

3. *Katha Upanishad* II 21–25.

4. Mukunda Rao (ed.), *The Biology of Enlightenment*.

5. Joseph Campbell, *Oriental Mythology*, London: Souvenir Press Ltd, 2000.

6. Many ancient myths of creation offer more or less the same kind of cosmology, that is, the world as emerging from the 'body' of the ancient one. So we cannot say the 'Indians' were foremost in arriving at such an interpretation of the origin of life. See, Mircea Eliade, *From Primitives to Zen: A Thematic Sourcebook of the History of Religions*, HarperCollins, 1978.

7. Joseph Campbell, *Oriental Mythology*.

8. Ibid.

9. *Majjhima Nikaya* 36.

10. Mukunda Rao (ed.), *The Biology of Enlightenment*.

11. Thich Nhat Hanh, *Old Path White Clouds: Walking in the Footsteps of the Buddha*, New Delhi: Full Circle, 2007.

12. Walpola Sri Rahula, *What the Buddha Taught*, Oxford: Oneworld Publications, 2007.

13. Sangharakshita, *A Survey of Buddhism: Its Doctrines and Methods through the Ages*, London: Tharpa Publications, 1987.

14. Walpola Sri Rahula, *What the Buddha Taught*.

15. D.T. Suzuki, *Studies in the Lankavatara Sutra*, Delhi: Motilal Banarsidass Publishers Pvt Ltd., 2007.

16. Munagala S. Venkataramiah, *Talks with Sri Ramana Maharshi*, Vols. I, II and III, Tiruvannamalai: Sri Ramanasramam, 1978.
17. Mukunda Rao (ed.), *The Biology of Enlightenment*.

The Biology of Nirvana

1. *Maitreya Upanishad* II, 5–9.
2. *Anguttara Nikaya* 55.
3. Pandit Gopi Krishna, *Living with Kundalini*, Boston: Shambala Publications, 1993; also see, Gopi Krishna, *What Is Cosmic Consciousness?* Connecticut: Bethel Publishers, 2004; Gopi Krishna, *Kundalini: Path to Higher Consciousness*, New Delhi: Orient Paperbacks, 1976; Gopi Krishna, *Kundalini: The Evolutionary Energy in Man*, with an introduction by Frederic Spiegelberg and a psychological commentary by James Hillman, London: Stuart & Watkins, 1970.
4. Pandit Gopi Krishna, *Living with Kundalini*.
5. Ibid.
6. Ibid.
7. Satprem, *The Mind of the Cells: Or Willed Mutation of Our Species*, New York: Institute For Evolutionary Research, 1982.
8. Ibid.
9. Ibid. Also see Kireet Joshi, *Sri Aurobindo and the Mother*, Delhi: The Mother's Institute of Research, in association with Motilal Banarsidass Publishers, 1996.
10. For a full report of the bodily changes U.G. Krishnamurti underwent and the nature of the 'natural state', in U.G. Krishnamurti's words, see Rodney Arms (ed.), *The Mystique of Enlightenment: The Unrational Ideas of a Man Called U.G.*, Goa: Dinesh Vaghela, 1982; Mukunda Rao (ed.), *The Biology of Enlightenment: Unpublished Conversations of U.G. Krishnamurti after He Came into the Natural State (1967–71)*, Noida, India: HarperCollins, 2010.
11. Mukunda Rao (ed.), *The Biology of Enlightenment*.
12. Rodney Arms (ed.), *The Mystique of Enlightenment*.

13. Arthur Osborne, *Ramana Maharshi and the Path of Self-Knowledge*, Tiruvannamalai: Sri Ramanasramam, 1997.

14. Ibid.

15. Ramana Maharishi, *Hridaya Vidya*, Tiruvannamalai, Sri Ramanasramam, 1997.

16. Rodney Arms (ed.), *The Mystique of Enlightenment*.

17. *Digha Nikaya* 30; *Majjhima Nikaya* 91. The thirty-two signs of mahapurusha lakshana parallel the physical changes U.G. Krishnamurti underwent after he came into the natural state in 1967. Spread over a week or two during the process of these biological changes U.G. Krishnamurti went through, some of his friends were witness to the following changes/marks:

> Up and down his torso, neck and head, at those points which the kundalini yoga calls chakras, his friends observed swellings of various shapes and colours, which came and went at intervals. On his lower abdomen the swellings were horizontal, cigar-shaped bands. Above the navel was a hard, almond-shaped swelling. A hard, blue swelling, like a large medallion, in the middle of his chest was surmounted by another smaller, brownish-red, medallion-shaped swelling at the base of his throat. These two 'medallions' were as though suspended from a varicolored, swollen ring, blue, brownish and light yellow, around his neck, as in pictures of the Hindu gods. There were also other similarities between the swellings and the depictions of Indian religious art: his throat was swollen to a shape that made his chin seem to rest on the head of a cobra, as in the traditional images of Siva; just above the bridge of the nose was a white lotus-shaped swelling; all over the head the small blood vessels expanded, forming patterns like the stylized lumps on the heads of Buddha statues. Like the horns of Moses and the Taoist mystics, two large, hard swellings periodically came and went. The arteries in his neck expanded and rose, blue and snake-like, into his head.

From Rodney Arms (ed.), *The Mystique of Enlightenment*. All this indicates that the sages in the past, including the Buddha, must have come upon such physical changes; perhaps they didn't talk about it in physical and physiological terms, or, what they said was subsumed under spiritual discourses, which were predominantly *anti-body* and framed in psychological terms.

18. Walpola Sri Rahula, *What the Buddha Taught*, Oxford: Oneworld Publications, 2007.

19. Lyall Watson, *Beyond Supernature: A New Natural History of the Supernatural*, New York: Bantam Books, 1988.

20. Mukunda Rao (ed.), *The Biology of Enlightenment*.

21. Walpola Sri Rahula, *What the Buddha Taught*.

22. Lyall Watson, *Beyond Supernature*; also see, Lyall Watson, *The Romeo Error: A Matter of Life and Death*, New York: Dell Publishing, 1976.

23. V.S. Ramachandran, *The Tell-Tale Brain: Unlocking the Mystery of Human Nature*, Delhi: Random House India, 2010.

BOOK TWO
Prajna-Paramita: The Perfection of Wisdom

The First Sermon

1. *Majjhima Nikaya* 1, 167.

2. Ibid.

3. T.R.V. Murti, *The Central Philosophy of Buddhism: A Study of Madhyamika System*, New Delhi: Munshiram Manoharlal Publishers Pvt. Ltd, 2010; also see, Harold G. Coward (ed.), *Studies in Indian Thought: Collected Papers of Prof. T.R.V. Murti*, Delhi: Motilal Banarsidass, 1983.

4. *Mahaparinirvana Sutra*, London: The Pali Text Society, 1971.

5. *Samyutta Nikaya* LVI, 11.

6. *Samyutta Nikaya* 35.

7. *Majjhima Nikaya* 69.

8. Walpola Sri Rahula, *What the Buddha Taught*, Oxford: Oneworld Publications, 2007.

9. Ibid.

Is There a Middle Path?

1. *Samyutta Nikaya* 56.11; *The Dhammacakkappavattana Sutta.*
2. T.R.V. Murti, *The Central Philosophy of Buddhism: A Study of Madhyamika System*, New Delhi: Munshiram Manoharlal Publishers Pvt. Ltd, 2010.
3. Stephen Metcalf (ed.), *Selected Writings: Friedrich Nietzsche*, New Delhi: Srishti Publishers & Distributors, 2001.
4. Arthur Koestler, *Janus: A Summing Up*, London: Hutchinson, 1979.
5. Edwin A. Burtt (ed.), *The Teachings of the Compassionate Buddha*, New York: Mentor Books, 1982.
6. T.R.V. Murti, *The Central Philosophy of Buddhism.*
7. *Digha Nikaya: Brahmajala Sutta* 27–28.
8. Mukunda Rao (ed.), *The Biology of Enlightenment: Unpublished Conversation of U.G. Krishnamurti after He Came into the Natural State (1967-71)*, Noida, India: HarperCollins, 2010.
9. *Majjhima Nikaya* 69.
10. Mukunda Rao (ed.), *The Biology of Enlightenment.*

Dukkha: The Birth of the Self

1. Edwin A. Burtt (ed.), *The Teachings of the Compassionate Buddha*, New York: Mentor Books, 1982.
2. *Majjhima Nikaya* 89.
3. Walpola Sri Rahula, *What the Buddha Taught*, Oxford: Oneworld Publications, 2007.
4. *Majjhima Nikaya* II, 32.
5. *J. Krishnamurti Talks and Dialogues*, Saanen, 3rd public talk, 11 July 1968.
6. *J. Krishnamurti Talks and Dialogues*, Saanen, July 1980.
7. Mukunda Rao (ed.), *The Biology of Enlightenment: Unpublished Conversations of U.G. Krishnamurti after He Came into the Natural State (1967–71)*, Noida, India: HarperCollins, 2010.
8. Upasaka Lu K'uan Yu (Charles Luk) trans., *Surangama Sutra*, London: Rider & Co., 1973.

Where is the Mind Located?

1. V.S. Ramachandran's Reith Lectures on 'The Emerging Mind' available online at http://www.bbc.couk/radio4/reith2003 (accessed on 22 March 2017).
2. V.S. Ramachandran, *The Tell-Tale Brain: Unlocking the Mystery of Human Nature*, Delhi: Random House India, 2010.
3. Fritjof Capra, *The Hidden Connection*, London: Flamingo, 2003.
4. Upasaka Lu K'uan Yu (Charles Luk) trans., *Surangama Sutra*, London: Rider & Co., 1973.
5. Ibid.
6. Ibid.
7. Mukunda Rao (ed.), *The Biology of Enlightenment: Unpublished Conversations of U.G. Krishnamurti after He Came into the Natural State (1967–71)*, Noida, India: HarperCollins, 2010. U.G. Krishnamurti's notion of the 'world mind' may be comparable to Carl Jung's concept of the 'collective unconscious' and the ancient idea of the akashic records.
8. Ibid.
9. *Majjhima Nikaya* 36.

No-Mind or Pure Consciousness

1. See *Mandukya Upanishad*.
2. Gaudapada, *Mandukya Karika* III, *Advaita Prakarana* 31–37.
3. *Talks with Sri Ramana Maharshi*, Vols. I, II and III, Tiruvannamalai: Sri Ramanasramam, 1978.
4. *Anguttara Nikaya* 5.28; *Samadhanga Sutta*, translated from the Pali by Thanissaro Bhikkhu at www.accesstoinsight.org (accessed on 22 March 2017).
5. Mukunda Rao (ed.), *The Biology of Enlightenment: Unpublished Conversations of U.G. Krishnamurti after He Came into the Natural State (1967–71)*, Noida, India: HarperCollins, 2010.
6. *Mundaka Upanishad* III, 1.

Is There a Soul?

1. *Majjhima Nikaya 69*.
2. Edward Conze (trans.), *Buddhist Scriptures*, England: Penguin Classics, 1959.
3. Mukunda Rao (ed.), *The Biology of Enlightenment: Unpublished Conversations of U.G. Krishnamurti after He Came into the Natural State (1967–71)*, Noida, India: HarperCollins, 2010.
4. Edward Conze (trans.), *Buddhist Scriptures*.

Is There Rebirth?

1. T.R.V. Murti, *The Central Philosophy of Buddhism: A Study of Madhyamika System*, New Delhi: Munshiram Manoharlal Publishers Pvt. Ltd, 2010.
2. T.W. Rhys Davids (trans.), *Dialogues of the Buddha*, Vols. 1, 2 and 3, London: The Pali Text Society, 1971–73.
3. T.R.V. Murti, *The Central Philosophy of Buddhism*.
4. S. Radhakrishnan, *Indian Philosophy*, Vol. 1, New Delhi: Oxford University Press, 1989.
5. Iqbal Singh, 'Gautama Buddha' in Matthew T. Kapstein (ed.), *The Buddhism Omnibus*, New Delhi: Oxford University Press, 2008.
6. Paul Carus, *Gospel of the Buddha*, Varanasi: Pilgrims Publishing, 2003.
7. Mukunda Rao (ed.), *The Biology of Enlightenment: Unpublished Conversations of U.G. Krishnamurti after He Came into the Natural State (1967–71)*, Noida, India: HarperCollins, 2010.
8. There is enough evidence to show that even after the person has stopped breathing and is declared dead, the brain is active for a while. For instance, in the famous case of Robert Kennedy, he survived seven minutes after actual clinical death. The brainwaves still continued after the heart and the pulse stopped. He was declared dead after the brainwaves ceased.

Sunyata

1. T.R.V. Murti, *The Central Philosophy of Buddhism: A Study of Madhyamika System*, New Delhi: Munshiram Manoharlal Publishers Pvt. Ltd, 2010.
2. Kenneth K. Inada (trans.), *Mulamadhyamaka Karika*, Tokyo: The Hokuseido Press, 1970.
3. For a very learned analysis and understanding of the notion of sunyata in the light of postmodern philosophy, see Ian W. Mabbett, 'Naagaarjuna and Deconstruction', *Philosophy East and West*, Vol. 45, No. 2, pp. 203–25, University of Hawaii Press; David R. Loy, 'The Deconstruction of Buddhism', in Coward and Foshay (eds), *Derrida and Negative Theology*, Suny Press, 1992; Steve Odin, 'Derrida and the Decentered Universe of Chan/Zen Buddhism', *Journal of Chinese Philosophy*, Vol. 17, 1990, pp. 61–86.
4. Mukunda Rao, *In Search of Shiva*, Bangalore: Dronequill, 2011.
5. Mukunda Rao (ed.), *The Penguin U.G. Krishnamurti Reader*, New Delhi: Penguin India, 2007.
6. *Samyutta Nikaya 35–85*; *Sunna Sutta*, translated from the Pali by Thanissaro Bhikkhu.
7. Mukunda Rao (ed.), *The Biology of Enlightenment: Unpublished Conversations of U.G. Krishnamurti after He Came into the Natural State (1967–71)*, Noida, India: HarperCollins, 2010.

The Silence of the Buddha

1. Edwin A. Burtt (ed.), *The Teachings of the Compassionate Buddha*, New York: Mentor Books, 1982.
2. David Godman (ed.), *Be As You Are: Teachings of Sri Ramana Maharshi*, New Delhi: Penguin Books, 1992.
3. Edwin A. Burtt, *The Teachings of the Compassionate Buddha*.
4. *Majjhima Nikaya 69*.
5. For a critical discussion of the meaning and significance of the Buddha's silence, see T.V.R. Murti, *The Central Philosophy of Buddhism: A Study of Madhyamika System*, New Delhi: Munshiram Manoharlal Publishers Pvt. Ltd, 2010.

6. Henry Clarke Warren, *Buddhism: In Translations*, New Delhi: Motilal Banarsidass Publishers, 2002.

7. *Samyutta Nikaya, 35–95; Malunkyaputta Sutta.*
   Translations from the Pali texts by Thanissaro Bhikkhu, Andrew Olendzki and Buddharakkhita are at www.accesstoinsight.org (accessed on 22 March 2017).

BOOK THREE
Mahasamadhi: The Final Absorption

Mahaparinirvana

1. T.W. Rhys Davids (trans.), *Mahaparinibbana Sutta*, London: The Pali Text Society, 1971.

2. Ibid.

3. Ibid.

4. Ibid.

5. T.W. Rhys Davids (trans.), *Mahaparinibbana Sutta.*

6. Bhikku Silacara, *Discourses of Gautama Buddha, The Buddha*, Vol. I, p. 41. There is an interesting parallel to this in the Gospel of Thomas: 14:
   > Jesus said to them, '... After all, what goes into your mouth will not defile you; rather, it's what comes out of your mouth that will defile you.'

7. Mukunda Rao, *The Other Side of Belief: Interpreting U.G. Krishnamurti*, New Delhi: Penguin India, 2005.

8. T.W. Rhys Davids (trans.), *Mahaparinibbana Sutta.*

9. Ibid.

10. S. Radhakrishnan, *Indian Philosophy*, Vol. 1, New Delhi: Oxford University Press, 1989.

The Way

1. Joseph Campbell, *Oriental Mythology*, London: Souvenir Press Ltd, 2000.

2.   Iqbal Singh, 'Gautama Buddha' in Matthew T. Kapstein (ed.), *The Buddhism Omnibus*, New Delhi: Oxford University Press, 2008.

3.   Joseph Campbell, *Oriental Mythology*.

4.   Walpola Sri Rahula, *What the Buddha Taught*, Oxford: Oneworld Publications, 2007.

5.   Karen Armstrong, *Buddha*, London: Phoenix, 2006.

6.   *Majjhima Nikaya* 69.

7.   Edwin A. Burtt (ed.), *The Teachings of the Compassionate Buddha*, New York: Mentor Books, 1982.

Also by Mukunda Rao

Fiction
Confessions of a Sanyasi (1988)
The Mahatma: A Novel (1992)
The Death of an Activist (1997)
Rama Revisited and Other Stories (2002)
Chinnamani's World (2003)
In Search of Shiva (2010)

Non-fiction
Babasaheb Ambedkar: Trials with Truth (2000)
The Other Side of Belief: Interpreting U.G. Krishnamurti (2005)
The Penguin U.G. Krishnamurti Reader (2007)
The Biology of Enlightenment: Unpublished Early Conversation of U.G. Krishnamurti After He Came Into the Natural State (1967–71)—Edited (2011)
Between the Serpent and the Rope: Ashrams, Traditions, Avatars, Sages and Con Artists (2014)

Plays
Mahatma: Khuda ka Hijra (1988 and 2009)
Babasaheb Ambedkar (2008 and 2014)